WILLIAMS-SONOMA

New American Cooking

The South

GENERAL EDITOR **Chuck Williams**

RECIPES AND TEXT **Ray Overton**

FOOD PHOTOGRAPHY **Leigh Beisch**

TIME
LIFE
BOOKS

New Ameri

The Pacific Northwest

California

The Southwes

Th

Table of **Contents**

Introduction

Close your eyes and think of the South. What do you see? You might conjure up visions of sprawling pasturelands, the occasional moss-covered oak tree, and huge, columned plantation homes. Or you might picture an unpaved rural road with a paint-starved country store where the locals stop to pick up their mail along with a bag of flour for making a batch of biscuits. Such places do still exist in pockets of the South, but there is a great deal more to the land we call Dixie and to the Southern cooking of today.

Contemporary Southern cooking could be humorously summed up as "something old, something new, something borrowed, and something roux." Its character is the result of the convergence of many factors: the classic cuisines and kitchen techniques of Africa, France, Spain, Great Britain, and the Caribbean mixed with the ingredients indigenous to the region. Today, innovative Southern chefs are combining stone-ground grits with goat cheese and topping them with spice-rubbed grilled shrimp and flash-fried okra, or serving pecan-crusted fried chicken with a molasses-drizzled sweet potato flan and stir-fried collard greens. Yet Southern suppers still carry an old-fashioned regional charm that beckons diners to loosen their belts and have another helping.

Butter-enriched Sally
Lunn Herbed Rolls (above)
improve almost any
Southern meal.

The Southern Table

Geography has strongly influenced
the Southern table. The Mason-Dixon
Line, born out of a disagreement
between two eighteenth-century
colonial families, separates Pennsyl-
vania from Maryland. In the years
before the Civil War, it was also
recognized as the dividing line
between the free and the slave
states. Everything south of the line
and bordered on the west by the
Mississippi River was known as
Dixie. During the Civil War, the
boundaries of the Confederate
states were redrawn to include
Arkansas, Louisiana, and Texas.

These demarcations shaped the
development of Southern cuisine.
Along the northern corridor of the
Mason-Dixon Line, the weather was
ideal for raising hogs, and pork
became the most prized meat in
the South. The middle South had
the perfect soil for growing the soft
wheat that was critical to making
light-as-air biscuits and flaky pie
crusts. In the Deep South, the long,
hot summers and rich earth guar-
anteed that tomatoes, green beans,
okra, melons, and sweet potatoes
were abundant. Peaches, peanuts,
and pecans rounded out the larder.
In bayou country, rustic French
recipes evolved into Cajun and
Creole cooking that incorporated
squashes, figs, rice, and the fish and

Duck (left) and other game once hunted are now commonly farm-raised throughout the South. Rice, also known as "Carolina gold," and crawfish (below) are two Southern mainstays.

shellfish from local waterways and the Gulf of Mexico.

African Influence

With the explosion of wealth and commerce in the eighteenth century came yet another important influence: the plantation lifestyle of

grand parties and elaborate meals. Such celebrations were possible, of course, only because of the slaves who worked the fields and in the kitchens of the great houses. Many African cooks learned to create imaginative dishes by mixing ingredients carried with them on the slave ships—black-eyed peas, sweet potatoes, okra, collard greens, watermelon, guinea hens, sesame seeds—with local foods—squashes and pumpkins, field peas and beans, ramps and wild onions, wild game from the forest, and seafood from the long coastline.

But it was politics as much as plantation life that shaped the character of Southern cooking. In 1865, with the end of the Civil War and slavery, whites and blacks alike fell on hard times, a period of poverty that would last a century. Soul food, that is, the survival cuisine the slaves had created, now evolved into a way of life for everyone. Former black slaves became the region's culinary teachers, instructing a struggling white society in how to survive on what little was available. These cooks knew how to use every part of the pig: the fat was rendered into lard for baking and deep-frying, the skin was fried into cracklings for flavoring breads and muffins; the intestines were stewed as chitterlings; the knuckles and feet were pickled; and the ham hocks and neck bones were stewed with greens. Soul food, born out of necessity, is perhaps the region's greatest culinary legacy.

Southern Hospitality

Pride in culinary pursuits, whether an old-fashioned pot of greens and ham hocks or a contemporary salad of smoked trout and fennel, is common in the South. Indeed, it seems as if nearly every Southerner is willing to wax on about what goes into a local dish and then invite a visitor to sit down and try a taste of it. But perhaps no other son of the South is

Collard greens and black-eyed peas (below), still popular in Southern cooking, carried the South through hard times.

more responsible for this legendary hospitality than Thomas Jefferson, the third president of the United States and one of the South's best-known "foodies." His plantation at Monticello, near Charlottesville, Virginia, included extensive gardens planted with countless fruit and vegetable varieties. He entertained lavishly, often playing host to as many as fifty dinner guests at one time. A score of dishes would be served and an endless stream of European wine, Antigua rum, and local hard cider would flow.

These affairs were more grand, more given to excess, and yet more relaxed than the dining rituals of the Puritans in the North, and this gregarious Southern hospitality has survived until today, even through the lean years of Reconstruction and the Great Depression. The main focus of Southern hospitality was and still is to get together with family and friends and share a meal.

A dear friend of mine tells me her beloved grandmother always had a batch of mouthwatering fried chicken

Old-Fashioned Vanilla Seed Pound Cake (left) and traditional desserts like it are as much a part of Southern hospitality as long chats and lemonade.

waiting for her no matter what time of day or night she arrived. This is Southern hospitality at its most basic and best, the sharing of wonderful foods with those we love. In this regard, little has changed over the years. Every time we make biscuits, simmer a mess of greens, or bake a pound cake, it is part of this long tradition. It is having our past, our present, and our hopes for the future all together on the dining room table that makes Southerners feel right at home.

13

1 Appetizers, Soups & Salads

This collection of starters uses some of the South's best-known foods: smoked brook trout, pecans, Atlantic coast crab, tart Key limes, plump Carolina shrimp, and oysters from the Gulf of Mexico. Familiar Southern vegetables take center stage, too, in such irresistible dishes as a puréed lima bean soup with smoked-ham croutons, a simple tart of Vidalia onions and root vegetables, and a thick chowder of black-eyed peas, rice, sweet potatoes, and greens. Although in the past these dishes, many of them lighter versions of traditional favorites, would have been served only as a first course, some Southerners today find themselves making a meal of two or three of them served together.

Pickled Pepper Shrimp with Okra

3 cups (24 fl oz/750 ml) cider vinegar

1 cup (8 fl oz/250 ml) fresh orange juice

1 cup (7 oz/220 g) firmly packed light brown sugar

2 Scotch bonnet chiles, seeded and thinly sliced

2 tablespoons coriander seeds, crushed

2 tablespoons mustard seeds

2 tablespoons dill seeds

1 tablespoon celery seeds

3 bay leaves, crumbled

12 peppercorns

6 allspice berries

2 teaspoons ground turmeric

2 teaspoons salt

3 lb (1.5 kg) large shrimp (prawns), peeled and deveined

1 lb (500 g) baby okra, no more than 2 inches (5 cm) long, stems trimmed without cutting into pod

1 Vidalia or other sweet onion, thinly sliced

1 red bell pepper and 1 green bell pepper (capsicum), seeded and thinly sliced lengthwise

1 lemon, thinly sliced

3 cloves garlic, chopped

½ cup (4 fl oz/125 ml) extra-virgin olive oil

24 baguette slices, toasted

A classic pickling, or preserving, method of the Deep South joins with the flavors of tropical Florida in this refreshing appetizer. Be sure to choose small, plump okra pods, or they will be tough and stringy when pickled.

1. In a large nonaluminum saucepan, stir together the vinegar, orange juice, brown sugar, chiles, coriander seeds, mustard seeds, dill seeds, celery seeds, bay leaves, peppercorns, allspice berries, turmeric, and salt. Bring to a boil over high heat, stirring to dissolve the sugar. Reduce the heat to low and simmer, uncovered, until the mixture is slightly reduced and very aromatic, about 10 minutes.

2. Add the shrimp, okra, onion, red and green bell peppers, lemon, and garlic. Return to a boil over high heat, remove from the heat, cover, and let cool to room temperature.

3. Stir the olive oil into the cooled mixture, transfer to a nonaluminum bowl, cover, and refrigerate for at least 8 hours or as long as 2 days, stirring occasionally.

4. Using a slotted spoon, transfer the shrimp and vegetables to small plates. Serve chilled or at room temperature with the baguette slices.

MAKES 3 QT (3 L); SERVES 12

NUTRITIONAL ANALYSIS PER SERVING
Calories 446 (Kilojoules 1,873); Protein 26 g; Carbohydrates 59 g; Total Fat 14 g; Saturated Fat 2 g; Cholesterol 140 mg; Sodium 845 mg; Dietary Fiber 4 g

Vidalia Onion and Root Vegetable Tart

pastry dough *(page 124)*

1 small sweet potato, peeled and shredded

1 small turnip, peeled and shredded

1 cup (4 oz/125 g) shredded sharp cheddar cheese

1 Vidalia or other sweet onion, thinly sliced

3 cloves garlic, chopped

½ cup (2½ oz/75 g) crumbled blue cheese

⅔ cup (5 fl oz/160 ml) heavy (double) cream

1 egg, lightly beaten

½ teaspoon salt

½ teaspoon ground white pepper

½ cup (2 oz/60 g) chopped pecans

½ cup (2 oz/60 g) grated Parmesan cheese

Vidalia onions are the pride and joy of south Georgia. Sweet and juicy, the pale yellow globes are so mild that some locals eat them out of hand, biting through the crisp layers as if eating apples. The natural sweetness of this legendary onion is highlighted in this simple savory tart.

1. Prepare the dough as directed. On a lightly floured work surface, roll out the dough into a thin round at least 11 inches (28 cm) in diameter and ⅛ inch (3 mm) thick. Fold the round into quarters and place in a 9-inch (23-cm) tart pan with a removable bottom. Unfold, then press gently into the bottom and sides of the pan. Trim the pastry even with the pan rim.

2. Preheat the oven to 375°F (190°C).

3. Mix together the shredded sweet potato and shredded turnip. Layer the vegetable mixture on the bottom of the tart crust. Top with the cheddar cheese. Slightly mound the onion slices and garlic over the cheese. Top evenly with the blue cheese.

4. In a small bowl, whisk together the cream, egg, salt, and white pepper. Slowly and evenly pour the mixture over the layers in the tart pan.

5. Bake for 25 minutes. Remove from the oven and top evenly with the pecans and then the Parmesan cheese. Return to the oven and continue baking until the tart is nicely browned, 25–30 minutes. If the edges begin to brown too quickly, lightly cover them with strips of aluminum foil. Transfer to a rack and let cool for at least 20 minutes.

6. Remove the pan sides and slide the tart off the base onto a serving platter. Cut into wedges and serve warm or at room temperature.

SERVES 8

NUTRITIONAL ANALYSIS PER SERVING
Calories 461 (Kilojoules 1,936); Protein 13 g; Carbohydrates 25 g; Total Fat 35 g; Saturated Fat 17 g; Cholesterol 96 mg; Sodium 662 mg; Dietary Fiber 2 g

It all started in the late spring of 1931, near the small south Georgia town of Vidalia. Mose Coleman, a local farmer, dug up his onions only to discover that his harvest was delicately sweet rather than the anticipated pungency. In time, however, he was able to sell his novelty crop at a good price. His success caught the attention of fellow farmers and soon everyone was growing sweet onions. The sweetness, it was later discovered, was the result of two primary factors: soil with a very low sulfur content and a growing season with high rainfall.

In the 1940s, the State of Georgia, recognizing the unusual onion's potential, built a farmers' market at Vidalia. It quickly sparked a booming tourist business from city folks out for a drive who wanted to take home some farm-fresh produce. Word spread and production grew steadily throughout the next three decades. Then, in 1986, the state legislature passed a bill granting legal status to the Vidalia onion and restricting its cultivation to a twenty-county area.

In the beginning, Vidalias were available only from late April through mid-June. Today, with storage technology borrowed from the apple

Sweet Vidalia **Onions**

industry, Vidalia growers have extended marketing through the fall and into the holiday season.

Vidalias, which range in size from small to jumbo, are somewhat flat, with golden brown skin. If you can't get your hands on Georgia's finest, you can substitute its rivals: the Maui, the Texas 1015 Supersweet, or the Walla Walla.

Crab Cakes with Key Lime Aioli

AIOLI

1 cup (8 fl oz/250 ml) mayonnaise

¼ cup (2 fl oz/60 ml) fresh Key lime juice

2 cloves garlic, chopped

1 tablespoon anchovy paste

2 teaspoons dry mustard

2 tablespoons chopped fresh parsley

2 tablespoons chopped fresh dill

salt and freshly ground pepper to taste

CRAB CAKES

1 tablespoon olive oil

1 small red bell pepper (capsicum), seeded and chopped

1 small yellow onion, chopped

2 cloves garlic, chopped

⅓ cup (3 fl oz/80 ml) mayonnaise

1 egg, lightly beaten

2 tablespoons fresh Key lime juice

2 teaspoons Jamaican jerk seasoning

1 teaspoon dry mustard

1 teaspoon paprika

1 lb (500 g) fresh-cooked lump crabmeat, picked over for shell fragments

salt and freshly ground pepper to taste

2 cups (8 oz/250 g) fine dried bread crumbs

vegetable oil for frying

Key lime slices

Blue crabs are plentiful along the eastern seaboard and the Gulf of Mexico. Their sweet meat makes wonderful crab cakes. These, made with Key lime juice and jerk seasoning, have an island flavor.

1. To make the aioli, in a food processor, combine the mayonnaise, lime juice, garlic, anchovy paste, and dry mustard. Process until smooth, about 1 minute. Transfer to a bowl and stir in the parsley, dill, salt, and pepper. Cover and refrigerate for at least 2 hours or as long as 2 days.

2. To make the crab cakes, in a frying pan over medium-high heat, warm the olive oil. Add the bell pepper, onion, and garlic and sauté until soft, about 5 minutes. Transfer to a bowl and stir in the mayonnaise, egg, lime juice, jerk seasoning, dry mustard, and paprika. Mix in the crabmeat, then season with salt and pepper. Add about 1 cup (4 oz/125 g) of the bread crumbs, mixing to make a nonsticky, doughlike consistency. Shape the mixture into 1-inch (2.5-cm) cakes.

3. Line a baking sheet with parchment (baking) paper. Spread the remaining bread crumbs on a plate, and roll the cakes in them, coating evenly. Place on the prepared baking sheet, cover, and refrigerate for 30 minutes.

4. In a large frying pan, pour in vegetable oil to a depth of 1 inch (2.5 cm) and heat to 360°F (180°C) on a deep-frying thermometer. Working in batches, place the cakes, one at a time, in the hot oil. Do not crowd the pan. Fry, turning once, until golden brown, about 1 minute on each side. Using a spatula or slotted spoon, transfer to paper towels to drain. Keep warm until all the crab cakes are cooked.

5. Arrange the crab cakes on a warmed serving platter and garnish with the lime slices. Pass the aioli at the table.

MAKES ABOUT 36 CRAB CAKES; SERVES 8

NUTRITIONAL ANALYSIS PER SERVING
Calories 540 (Kilojoules 2,268); Protein 17 g; Carbohydrates 25 g; Total Fat 41 g; Saturated Fat 6 g; Cholesterol 106 mg; Sodium 730 mg; Dietary Fiber 2 g

Gulf Oyster Stew

2 pt (1 l) freshly shucked Apalachicola or Blue Point oysters

1 cup (3 oz/90 g) sliced fresh button mushrooms

3 cups (24 fl oz/750 ml) chicken stock

4 cups (32 fl oz/1 l) half-and-half (half cream)

1 tablespoon unsalted butter

dash of Tabasco or other hot-pepper sauce

1 teaspoon freshly cracked pepper

salt to taste

1 cup (1½ oz/45 g) tightly packed spinach leaves, tough stems removed

1 tablespoon bourbon (optional)

1 tablespoon chopped fresh tarragon

paprika

Apalachicola, Florida, produces some of the sweetest, most succulent oysters in the world, and this stew is one of my favorite ways to enjoy them. In the South, freshly shucked oysters are sold by the pint (500 ml). Brief, gentle simmering is the key to keeping their pleasantly briny flavor alive in this rich broth.

1. Drain the oysters, reserving the liquor. Set the oysters aside.

2. In a large saucepan over high heat, combine the oyster liquor, mushrooms, and chicken stock. Bring to a boil and boil until the liquid is reduced by about one-third, about 5 minutes. Reduce the heat to low and add the half-and-half, butter, Tabasco, pepper, and salt. Simmer very gently, uncovered, stirring occasionally, for about 20 minutes. Do not allow to boil.

3. Meanwhile, stack 10–12 spinach leaves, roll up into a tight cylinder, and thinly slice on the diagonal to make a chiffonade. Repeat with the remaining leaves.

4. When the stew base is ready, stir in the drained oysters and the bourbon, if using. Cook over low heat until the oysters just begin to curl around the edges, about 3 minutes. Stir in the spinach, cover, and remove from the heat to allow the spinach to wilt, about 2 minutes. Stir in the tarragon. Taste and adjust the seasonings.

5. Ladle into warmed bowls and lightly dust each serving with paprika.

SERVES 6

NUTRITIONAL ANALYSIS PER SERVING
Calories 363 (Kilojoules 1,525); Protein 18 g; Carbohydrates 15 g; Total Fat 26 g; Saturated Fat 14 g; Cholesterol 157 mg; Sodium 761 mg; Dietary Fiber 0 g

Hoppin' John Chowder

Here I've added turnip greens to Hoppin' John, a bean-and-rice dish traditionally prepared by Southern cooks for New Year's Day. The black-eyed peas are said to represent the Civil War's fallen Confederate soldiers, while eating turnip greens on January 1 ensures prosperity in the coming year.

1. In a large saucepan over medium heat, cook the bacon until some of the fat is rendered, about 2 minutes. Add the onion and garlic and cook, stirring, until tender, 5 minutes.

2. Drain the tomatoes, reserving the juice, and chop coarsely. Add the tomatoes and juice, sweet potato, black-eyed peas, turnip greens, rice, chicken stock, vinegar, cumin, salt, and pepper. Bring to a boil, cover, reduce the heat to low, and simmer until the sweet potato and rice are tender, about 40 minutes.

3. Stir in the parsley and ladle into warmed bowls. Serve immediately.

SERVES 6–8

NUTRITIONAL ANALYSIS PER SERVING
Calories 258 (Kilojoules 1,084); Protein 10 g; Carbohydrates 41 g; Total Fat 7 g;
Saturated Fat 2 g; Cholesterol 4 mg; Sodium 1,325 mg; Dietary Fiber 5 g

2 slices bacon, coarsely chopped

1 Vidalia or other sweet onion, chopped

2 cloves garlic, chopped

1 can (1 lb/500 g) whole tomatoes with juice

1 sweet potato, peeled and cut into ½-inch (12-mm) dice

2 lb (1 kg) fresh black-eyed peas, shelled, about 2 cups, or 1 bag (1 lb/500 g) frozen black-eyed peas, thawed

1 lb (500 g) turnip greens, tough stems removed and leaves coarsely chopped

½ cup (3½ oz/105 g) long-grained white rice

8 cups (64 fl oz/2 l) chicken stock, preferably homemade

¼ cup (2 fl oz/60 ml) cider vinegar

2 teaspoons ground cumin

salt and freshly ground pepper to taste

1 tablespoon chopped fresh parsley

Silken Lima Bean Soup with Ham Croûtes

SOUP

4 lb (2 kg) fresh limas, shelled (about 4 cups), or 2 bags (1 lb/500 g each) frozen lima beans, thawed

8 cups (64 fl oz/2 l) chicken stock

1 russet potato, peeled and cut into ½-inch (12-mm) dice

1 yellow onion, chopped

2 cloves garlic, chopped

1 carrot, peeled and chopped

½ teaspoon salt

½ teaspoon freshly ground pepper

½ cup (4 fl oz/125 ml) heavy (double) cream

1 tablespoon fresh thyme leaves

CROÛTES

6 slices French bread, each 1 inch (2.5 cm) thick

½ cup (3 oz/90 g) chopped country ham

⅓ cup (1½ oz/45 g) shredded cheddar cheese

2 tablespoons cream cheese, at room temperature

1 tablespoon mayonnaise

freshly ground pepper to taste

Lima beans grow in gardens all over the South and are available fresh from June to September. Fordhooks, my favorite variety, are larger and have a fuller flavor than those known as baby limas. If using fresh beans, choose pods that are firm, plump, and dark green, and shell them just before cooking.

1. To make the soup, in a large saucepan over high heat, combine the lima beans, chicken stock, potato, onion, garlic, carrot, salt, and pepper. Bring to a boil, reduce the heat to low, cover partially, and cook, stirring occasionally, until the vegetables are very soft, about 1 hour.

2. Meanwhile, make the croûtes: Preheat the oven to 400°F (200°C). Arrange the bread slices on a baking sheet and toast until golden brown, about 10 minutes. Remove from the oven and turn the oven to broil (grill). Position a rack 6 inches (15 cm) from the heat source.

3. In a small bowl, stir together the ham, cheddar cheese, cream cheese, mayonnaise, and pepper. Divide among the bread slices and spread evenly.

4. When the soup is ready, ladle it into a food processor, in batches if necessary, and purée until smooth. Return the purée to the saucepan and stir in the cream.

5. While the soup is reheating, broil (grill) the croûtes until the topping is bubbly and golden, about 2 minutes.

6. Ladle the soup into warmed bowls, sprinkle with the thyme leaves, and serve the croûtes on the side.

SERVES 6

NUTRITIONAL ANALYSIS PER SERVING
Calories 547 (Kilojoules 2,297); Protein 25 g; Carbohydrates 68 g; Total Fat 20 g; Saturated Fat 9 g; Cholesterol 51 mg; Sodium 2,311 mg; Dietary Fiber 8 g

Mississippi Caviar

4 lb (2 kg) fresh black-eyed peas, shelled, about 4 cups, or 2 bags (1 lb/500 g each) frozen black-eyed peas, thawed

1 ear of yellow or Silver Queen corn, husks and silk removed

3 slices bacon, coarsely chopped

1 small red (Spanish) onion, chopped

2 cloves garlic, chopped

⅓ cup (3 fl oz/80 ml) cider vinegar

1 tablespoon sugar

2 plum (Roma) tomatoes, seeded and coarsely chopped

1 cucumber, halved lengthwise, seeded, and finely diced

1 teaspoon Tabasco or other hot-pepper sauce

juice of 1 lime

2 teaspoons ground cumin

1 teaspoon ground coriander

salt and freshly ground pepper to taste

2 green (spring) onions, white and tender green parts only, minced

After the Civil War, many Southerners found that black-eyed peas were among the very few foods available. They nicknamed them caviar, indicating just how precious these very ordinary beans had become. This contemporary recipe has a fiery kick. Serve it as an appetizer with crisp tortilla chips.

1. If using fresh peas, bring a large pot three-fourths full of salted water to a boil over high heat. Add the peas and boil until just tender, about 35 minutes. Drain and set aside.

2. Holding the ear of corn by its pointed end and steadying its stalk end on a cutting board, cut down along the ear with a sharp knife, stripping off the kernels and rotating the ear with each cut. Set aside.

3. In a large frying pan over medium-high heat, fry the bacon until crisp and golden brown, about 5 minutes. Using a slotted spoon, transfer to paper towels to drain.

4. Reduce the heat to medium and add the red onion, garlic, and corn kernels to the hot drippings. Cook, stirring often, until the vegetables are tender, about 5 minutes. Stir in the vinegar and sugar and continue cooking until the liquid evaporates, about 3 minutes.

5. Transfer the contents of the frying pan to a large bowl. Add the black-eyed peas and mix well. Then stir in the tomatoes, cucumber, Tabasco, lime juice, cumin, coriander, salt, and pepper. Crumble in the reserved bacon, toss to mix thoroughly, cover, and refrigerate for at least 4 hours or as long as overnight.

6. Top with the green onions just before serving. Serve chilled or at room temperature.

SERVES 6

NUTRITIONAL ANALYSIS PER SERVING
Calories 125 (Kilojoules 525); Protein 6 g; Carbohydrates 18 g; Total Fat 4 g; Saturated Fat 1 g; Cholesterol 4 mg; Sodium 112 mg; Dietary Fiber 3 g

Southerners have a love affair with hot-pepper sauces. They drizzle them on everything from scrambled eggs and skillet corn bread to greens, gumbos, and, for the most die-hard fans, ice cream.

Why would any region with summertime temperatures hot enough to make even the preacher's wife cranky crave fiery foods? It all has to do with capsaicin, the potent, heat-producing chemical present in chiles. In addition to causing a burning sensation, capsaicin, we now know, triggers the brain to release endorphins, natural painkillers that promote a sense of well-being. It also encourages us to perspire, cooling us internally even on a midsummer scorcher.

Capsaicin survives cooking and pickling, and it is in pickling that the South's beloved pepper sauces are born. Arguably the most famous of the lot is Tabasco, which was developed shortly after the Civil War by Edmund McIlhenny. He obtained chile seeds from a Central American traveler passing through Louisiana, planted them on Avery Island, a salt dome just off the Louisiana Gulf coast, harvested the crop, and then experimented until he hit upon a

Hot-Pepper **Sauces**

sauce he liked. The recipe has not changed in over a century: The day the peppers are picked, they are mashed, mixed with Avery Island salt, placed in barrels, and left to ferment and age for three years. The mash is then blended with vinegar and, about a month later, strained, bottled, and sold in 105 countries around the world.

Smoked Trout, Fennel, and Apple Salad

VINAIGRETTE

½ cup (2 oz/60 g) chopped pecans

⅓ cup (3 fl oz/80 ml) apple cider

¼ cup (2 fl oz/60 ml) fresh lemon juice

1 tablespoon prepared horseradish

2 teaspoons coarse-grain Dijon mustard

1 clove garlic, chopped

1 tablespoon brine-packed green peppercorns, rinsed and drained

Tabasco or other hot-pepper sauce to taste

⅓ cup (3 fl oz/80 ml) extra-virgin olive oil

1 teaspoon sugar

½ teaspoon salt

½ teaspoon freshly ground black pepper

SALAD

1 tart apple such as Granny Smith

1 tablespoon fresh lemon juice

1 whole smoked trout, 12–16 oz (375–500 g)

1 fennel bulb

1 Vidalia or other sweet onion, thinly sliced

1 red bell pepper (capsicum), seeded and thinly sliced lengthwise

1 tablespoon chopped fresh tarragon

2 green (spring) onions, tender green tops included, chopped

In late fall, homegrown apples fill the farm stands in north Georgia, making this an ideal seasonal salad. Serve it with a brisk, buttery Chardonnay and crisp bread sticks.

1. To make the vinaigrette, preheat the oven to 400°F (200°C). Spread the pecans on a baking sheet and toast until lightly browned and aromatic, about 8 minutes. Remove from the oven and let cool.

2. In a small bowl, stir together the apple cider, lemon juice, horseradish, mustard, garlic, green peppercorns, and Tabasco until blended. Whisk in the olive oil until thoroughly combined. Add the sugar, salt, black pepper, and toasted pecans. Taste and adjust the seasonings.

3. To make the salad, halve the unpeeled apple, core, and thinly slice crosswise. Place in a bowl, add the lemon juice, and toss to coat.

4. Remove the head, skin, and fins of the smoked trout, then carefully lift off each fillet from the backbone. With a fork, flake the fish into bite-sized pieces, removing and discarding any smaller bones. Add to the bowl with the apple.

5. Cut off the stems and feathery tops and any bruised outer stalks from the fennel bulb, then halve lengthwise and remove the core. Thinly slice crosswise. Add to the trout and apple along with the sweet onion, bell pepper, and tarragon.

6. Pour the vinaigrette over the salad and toss gently to coat completely. Let stand at room temperature for 30 minutes to allow the flavors to mingle.

7. Just before serving, toss the salad once again. Divide the tossed salad among individual plates. Sprinkle with the green onions and serve.

SERVES 4

NUTRITIONAL ANALYSIS PER SERVING
Calories 437 (Kilojoules 1,835); Protein 15 g; Carbohydrates 26 g; Total Fat 33 g; Saturated Fat 5 g; Cholesterol 11 mg; Sodium 959 mg; Dietary Fiber 5 g

Crisp Summer Salad

DRESSING

½ cup (4 fl oz/125 ml) cider vinegar

2 tablespoons Asian sesame oil

1 tablespoon peeled and chopped
   fresh ginger

2 cloves garlic, chopped

¼ cup (¾ oz/20 g) sesame seeds

2 tablespoons sugar

2 teaspoons dry mustard

¼ teaspoon red pepper flakes

SALAD

2 large cucumbers

1 Vidalia or other sweet onion, thinly
   sliced

1 green bell pepper (capsicum), seeded
   and thinly sliced crosswise

1 cup (5 oz/155 g) sliced radishes

salt and freshly ground black pepper
   to taste

¼ cup (⅓ oz/10 g) chopped fresh
   mint

In summer, cucumbers, bell peppers, and radishes, fresh from the garden, make a wonderfully crisp salad. In winter, you can substitute roasted or steamed beets for the cucumbers. The dressing also makes a nice marinade for chicken, pork, or fish.

1. To make the dressing, in a small bowl or a small jar with a tight-fitting lid, combine the vinegar, sesame oil, ginger, garlic, sesame seeds, sugar, dry mustard, and red pepper flakes. Whisk or shake until well blended.

2. To make the salad, peel the cucumbers. Cut them in half lengthwise and scoop out the seeds with a spoon. Slice thinly on the diagonal into crescents.

3. In a large bowl, combine the cucumbers, onion, bell pepper, and radishes. Drizzle on the dressing and toss to coat evenly. Season with salt and black pepper. Cover and refrigerate for at least 1 hour or as long as 8 hours before serving.

4. When ready to serve, toss again and divide the salad among individual plates. Garnish with the mint and serve.

SERVES 6

NUTRITIONAL ANALYSIS PER SERVING
Calories 134 (Kilojoules 563); Protein 3 g; Carbohydrates 18 g; Total Fat 7 g;
Saturated Fat 1 g; Cholesterol 0 mg; Sodium 21 mg; Dietary Fiber 3 g

Vine-Ripened Tomato and Corn Salad

Nothing embodies summer in the Deep South more than a bite from a just-picked ruby red tomato, still warm from the hot July sun, or the sweet taste of fresh corn. This salad, for all its simplicity, is a winner every time, whether enjoyed as a first course or a light lunch.

1. Have ready a large bowl of ice water. Bring a saucepan three-fourths full of lightly salted water to a boil. Add the corn and cook for 3 minutes. Using tongs, transfer the corn to the ice water to stop the cooking.

2. When the corn is cool, drain and pat dry. Holding an ear by its pointed end and steadying its stalk end on a cutting board, cut down along the ear with a sharp knife, stripping off the kernels and rotating the ear with each cut. Repeat with the remaining ear.

3. On a large, round plate, arrange the tomato slices in concentric circles, overlapping them. Scatter the corn kernels and green onions over the tomatoes. Drizzle with the olive oil and balsamic vinegar, and season with salt and pepper. Scatter the feta cheese and thyme leaves on top.

4. Garnish with the thyme sprigs and serve at room temperature.

SERVES 4

NUTRITIONAL ANALYSIS PER SERVING
Calories 208 (Kilojoules 874); Protein 6 g; Carbohydrates 23 g; Total Fat 12 g;
Saturated Fat 4 g; Cholesterol 16 mg; Sodium 229 mg; Dietary Fiber 5 g

2 ears of yellow or Silver Queen corn, husks and silk removed

4 large, very ripe tomatoes, cut into slices ¼ inch (6 mm) thick

3 green (spring) onions, white and tender green parts only, chopped

2 tablespoons extra-virgin olive oil

2 tablespoons balsamic vinegar

salt and freshly ground pepper to taste

½ cup (2½ oz/75 g) crumbled feta cheese

1 tablespoon fresh thyme leaves, plus sprigs for garnish

Cheddar–Benne Seed Wafers

1½ cups (7½ oz/235 g) all-purpose (plain) flour

1 cup (4 oz/125 g) grated Parmesan cheese

1 cup (4 oz/125 g) shredded sharp cheddar cheese

⅓ cup (1 oz/30 g) sesame seeds

1 teaspoon ground cumin

½ teaspoon salt

¼ teaspoon cayenne pepper

½ cup (4 oz/125 g) plus 2 tablespoons chilled unsalted butter, cut into ½-inch (12-mm) cubes

Sesame seeds were first brought to the New World on slave ships, and many Southerners still call them by their African name, benne. Serve these crackers with drinks before dinner.

1. In a food processor, combine the flour, Parmesan cheese, cheddar cheese, sesame seeds, cumin, salt, cayenne pepper, and butter. Process until the mixture is well combined but crumbly and holds together when squeezed with your hand, about 2 minutes.

2. Transfer to a lightly floured work surface and knead gently until the dough comes together and holds its shape. Then, using your hands, roll the dough into a log about 12 inches (30 cm) long and about 1½ inches (4 cm) in diameter. Wrap in plastic wrap and refrigerate until firm, at least 3 hours or as long as 24 hours. (At this point, the logs can be tightly wrapped in plastic wrap, then covered with heavy-duty aluminum foil and frozen for up to 3 months. Slice and bake directly from the freezer, allowing an additional 2 minutes baking time.)

3. Preheat the oven to 375°F (190°C). Line 2 baking sheets with parchment (baking) paper.

4. Remove the dough from the refrigerator and quickly cut into slices ¼ inch (6 mm) thick. Arrange the slices about 1 inch (2.5 cm) apart on the prepared baking sheets.

5. Bake until the edges appear crisp and brown, about 10 minutes. Let cool on the baking sheets for about 2 minutes, then transfer the wafers to wire racks to cool completely. They can be stored in an airtight container for up to 1 week.

MAKES ABOUT 4 DOZEN WAFERS

NUTRITIONAL ANALYSIS PER WAFER
Calories 62 (Kilojoules 260); Protein 2 g; Carbohydrates 4 g; Total Fat 4 g; Saturated Fat 2 g; Cholesterol 11 mg; Sodium 83 mg; Dietary Fiber 0 g

FARM
USE

VIDALIA
SWEET ONIONS
99 LB

2 Seafood, Poultry & Meats

In the new Southern kitchen, local meats, poultry, and seafood provide the centerpiece of the meal, just as they did in the rich and opulent days of Thomas Jefferson. In the hard-scrabble years after the Civil War, these same foods were a luxury, reserved for such special occasions as Christmas or when the preacher came to call. Nowadays, Southern main courses can be as simple as fried chicken or country ham or as elegant as peach-basted pork chops or beef fillets with a bourbon-mushroom glaze.

Buttermilk-Cornmeal Fried Chicken

2 cups (16 fl oz/500 ml) buttermilk

1 teaspoon Tabasco or other hot-pepper sauce

1 frying chicken, about 4 lb (2 kg), cut into 8 serving pieces

1 cup (5 oz/155 g) yellow cornmeal

1 cup (5 oz/155 g) all-purpose (plain) flour

1 teaspoon salt

1 teaspoon freshly ground pepper

1 teaspoon chopped fresh sage

½ teaspoon paprika

½ teaspoon garlic powder

½ teaspoon onion powder

2 cups (1 lb/500 g) solid vegetable shortening

Ask Southerners to name their favorite dish and the answer is inevitably fried chicken. There are probably as many recipes for this Southern specialty as there are folks to enjoy it. My version uses buttermilk and Tabasco to tenderize and flavor the chicken, and cornmeal for a crisp crust.

1. In a large bowl, stir together the buttermilk and Tabasco. Slip the chicken pieces into the mixture. Cover and refrigerate for at least 4 hours or as long as overnight.

2. In a shallow baking dish, stir together the cornmeal, flour, salt, pepper, sage, paprika, garlic powder, and onion powder. Remove each piece of chicken from the buttermilk, allowing the excess to drip away. Coat the chicken pieces evenly with the seasoned flour and place on a large baking sheet.

3. In a large, deep frying pan over medium-high heat, melt the shortening and heat to 360°F (180°C) on a deep-frying thermometer. Arrange the chicken, skin side down, in the pan, placing the pieces of dark meat in the center and the pieces of white meat around the sides. Allow the pieces to touch slightly, but do not overcrowd the pan. Reduce the heat to medium and cook until golden brown, about 12 minutes. Using tongs, turn the chicken, cover, and continue to cook for 10 minutes. Uncover, turn the chicken once more, and cook until crisp and cooked through, about 10 minutes longer.

4. Using tongs, transfer to paper towels to drain. Serve piping hot, at room temperature, or even chilled, straight from the refrigerator.

SERVES 4

NUTRITIONAL ANALYSIS PER SERVING
Calories 884 (Kilojoules 3,713); Protein 60 g; Carbohydrates 37 g; Total Fat 54 g; Saturated Fat 14 g; Cholesterol 178 mg; Sodium 595 mg; Dietary Fiber 2 g

Country-Fried Steak with Vidalia Onion Gravy

4 pieces round steak, ½ lb (250 g) each, trimmed of visible fat

1 cup (5 oz/155 g) all-purpose (plain) flour

2 tablespoons cornstarch (cornflour)

1 teaspoon onion powder

1 teaspoon garlic powder

½ teaspoon salt

½ teaspoon freshly ground black pepper

¼ teaspoon cayenne pepper

2 tablespoons unsalted butter

2 tablespoons olive oil

3 Vidalia or other sweet onions, thinly sliced

2 cups (16 fl oz/500 ml) beef stock

1 cup (8 fl oz/250 ml) milk

Here is a simple recipe that shows off the Southerner's love for gravy—on everything.

1. Using a meat pounder, pound the steaks until slightly flattened and uniform in thickness.

2. In a large lock-top plastic bag, combine the flour, cornstarch, onion powder, garlic powder, salt, black pepper, and cayenne pepper. Seal closed and shake the bag to mix. Remove ⅓ cup (2 oz/60 g) of the seasoned flour mixture and set aside. Add the pounded steaks, one at a time, to the bag. Seal and shake the bag to coat the steaks evenly.

3. In a large frying pan over medium-high heat, melt the butter with the olive oil. Reduce the heat to medium, add the steaks, and cook, turning once, until well browned, about 4 minutes on each side. Transfer to a plate and tent with aluminum foil to keep warm.

4. Add the onions to the pan over medium heat and cook, stirring often, until they begin to soften, 5–7 minutes. Stir in the reserved ⅓ cup (2 oz/60 g) seasoned flour and cook, stirring often, for 1 minute. Add the beef stock and milk, bring quickly to a boil, stirring constantly, and deglaze the pan, stirring to remove any browned bits from the pan bottom. Reduce the heat to low, stir in any accumulated juices from the browned steaks, and then nestle the meat into the simmering gravy.

5. Cover and simmer over very low heat, stirring occasionally, until the gravy is very thick and the meat is fork tender, about 45 minutes. Taste and adjust the seasonings.

6. Transfer to warmed individual plates and serve at once.

SERVES 4

NUTRITIONAL ANALYSIS PER SERVING
Calories 835 (Kilojoules 3,507); Protein 61 g; Carbohydrates 59 g; Total Fat 39 g; Saturated Fat 14 g; Cholesterol 173 mg; Sodium 889 mg; Dietary Fiber 5 g

Louisiana Crawfish Boil

4–6 oz (125–185 g) packaged crab and crawfish boil or Creole seasoning

1–2 tablespoons cayenne pepper (optional)

3 bay leaves

1 lemon, sliced

1 cup (8 fl oz/250 ml) cider vinegar

18 lb (9 kg) crawfish in the shell

18 small new potatoes

6 ears of yellow corn, husks and silk removed and ears halved

A crawfish boil is to the South what a clambake is to the Northeast. This feast is ideal for a casual gathering of friends who know one another well enough to dive into a heaping mound of steaming crawfish, corn, and potatoes with bare fingers and good appetites. Serve with lots of napkins, cocktail sauce and clarified butter for dipping, and ice-cold beer.

1. Fill a very large stockpot about two-thirds full with water. Add the seasoning, cayenne pepper to taste (if using), bay leaves, lemon slices, and vinegar and bring to a boil over high heat. Add about one-third of the crawfish. Bring back to a boil and cook until the crawfish are firm and bright, about 3 minutes. Using a slotted spoon, transfer to a large, clean bowl and cover. Repeat with the remaining crawfish in two more batches, adding them to the bowl as they are done.

2. Add the potatoes to the boiling water and cook for 15 minutes. Add the corn and continue cooking until the corn is just tender, about 4 minutes longer. Using the slotted spoon, transfer the potatoes and corn to another bowl.

3. Heap the cooked crawfish onto several large serving platters (or cover a picnic table with newspapers for dining al fresco). Serve with the potatoes and corn.

SERVES 6

NUTRITIONAL ANALYSIS PER SERVING
Calories 575 (Kilojoules 2,415); Protein 63 g; Carbohydrates 70 g; Total Fat 5 g; Saturated Fat 1 g; Cholesterol 404 mg; Sodium 1,034 mg; Dietary Fiber 8 g

According to legend, rice cultivation in South Carolina began in 1620, when the captain of a British merchant ship that sailed into Charleston from Madagascar gave his plantation-owner host a handful of so-called Golde Seede Rice. The plantation fields were flat, fertile, and well irrigated—ideal conditions for rice production. By the early 1700s, rice was a major crop in South Carolina, and the port of Charleston was exporting huge shiploads of Carolina Golde to England annually. By the mid-1800s, rice production began to move west to Mississippi, Louisiana, Arkansas, and Texas. Today, these states produce almost 80 percent of the rice eaten in the United States.

A second legend—an old wives' tale actually—accounts for another famous Southern food. When the Acadians, later known as Cajuns, left Nova Scotia for Louisiana, a school of lobsters followed. The lobsters molted repeatedly during the long journey, so that by the time they reached Louisiana, they had become the tiny morsels known affectionately as crawfish, crayfish, crawdads, or mudbugs.

Although crawfish look like miniature lobsters, these tasty freshwater

Rice and **Crawfish**

denizens are only distant cousins. Today most crawfish are farm raised, with the harvest beginning in December and lasting until May or June. After the rice harvest, some ambitious farmers seed their fields with crawfish eggs, knowing they will hatch and feed on the rice stubble that is left behind, producing a second cash crop for the season.

Rack of Lamb with Fig-Port Sauce

½ cup (4 fl oz/125 ml) chicken stock

⅔ cup (3 oz/90 g) dried bread crumbs

4 cloves garlic, chopped

3 tablespoons chopped fresh rosemary

3 tablespoons coriander seeds, crushed

2 tablespoons Dijon mustard

1 teaspoon dry mustard

1 teaspoon mustard seeds

salt and freshly ground pepper to taste

2 racks of lamb, each 1½–1¾ lb (750–875 g) with 7 ribs, trimmed of visible fat

1½ cups (12 fl oz/375 ml) dry white wine

SAUCE

½ cup (5 oz/155 g) fig preserves

⅓ cup (3 fl oz/80 ml) ruby port

2 tablespoons fresh lemon juice

1 tablespoon balsamic vinegar

2 teaspoons Dijon mustard

3 tablespoons chilled unsalted butter

3 tablespoons chopped fresh mint

Cajun cooks of the backwater bayous traditionally served a variation of the sauce used here with pork. It is wonderful on lamb, especially the excellent spring lamb from Kentucky. Ask your butcher to "french" the rack for you, which means trimming the meat from the ends of the bone.

1. In a small bowl, stir together the chicken stock, bread crumbs, garlic, rosemary, coriander seeds, Dijon mustard, dry mustard, mustard seeds, salt, and pepper. Pat the paste all over the meat. Cover and refrigerate for about 2 hours.

2. Place the racks, curve downward, in a baking pan. Let stand at room temperature for 1 hour. Preheat the oven to 450°F (230°C).

3. Pour the wine around the lamb. Cook until an instant-read thermometer inserted into the meatiest part of the lamb away from the bone registers 125°–130°F (52°–54°C) for rare, 20–25 minutes, or until done to your liking. Transfer the lamb to a warmed platter and tent with aluminum foil to keep warm. Reserve the pan juices.

4. To make the sauce, in a saucepan over medium-high heat, stir together the fig preserves, port, lemon juice, vinegar, mustard, and the pan juices. Bring to a boil and boil until the sauce begins to thicken, about 5 minutes. Remove from the heat and pour through a sieve into a warmed bowl. Whisk in the butter, 1 tablespoon at a time, until the sauce is glossy and smooth. Stir in the mint and taste and adjust the seasonings.

5. Cut the lamb racks into individual chops. Divide the sauce among warmed individual plates. Overlap 3 lamb chops per person on each plate. (The 2 end pieces are the cook's treat!) Serve immediately.

SERVES 4

NUTRITIONAL ANALYSIS PER SERVING
Calories 590 (Kilojoules 2,478); Protein 36 g; Carbohydrates 46 g; Total Fat 26 g; Saturated Fat 11 g; Cholesterol 128 mg; Sodium 688 mg; Dietary Fiber 4 g

Roast Chicken with Cider and Molasses

GLAZE

3 cups (24 fl oz/750 ml) apple cider

½ cup (5½ oz/170 g) dark molasses

¼ cup (2 fl oz/60 ml) cider vinegar

½ cup (¾ oz/20 g) chopped mixed
    fresh herbs such as parsley, rose-
    mary, tarragon, oregano, and basil,
    in any combination

3 tablespoons unsalted butter

3 tablespoons olive oil

2 Vidalia or other sweet onions,
    quartered

12 cloves garlic, peeled but left whole

1 roasting chicken, about 5 lb (2.5 kg)

2 cups (16 fl oz/500 ml) chicken
    stock

1 cup (8 fl oz/250 ml) dry red wine

½ cup (¾ oz/20 g) chopped mixed
    fresh herbs, as for the glaze

salt and freshly ground pepper
    to taste

This was our family's standard "company Sunday dinner,"
reserved for when the preacher and his wife came by.

1. To make the glaze, in a saucepan, bring the apple cider to a boil over high heat. Reduce the heat to medium and boil constantly until syrupy and reduced to about ½ cup (4 fl oz/125 ml), about 45 minutes. Remove from the heat and stir in the molasses, vinegar, and herbs. Set aside.

2. Preheat the oven to 450°F (230°C). In a frying pan over medium heat, melt the butter with the olive oil. Add the onions and garlic and cook, stirring often, until lightly browned, about 15 minutes; reserve.

3. Rinse the chicken and pat dry. Place, breast side up, in a roasting pan. Using a slotted spoon, transfer the onions and garlic to the cavity. Reserve the fat in the frying pan. Truss the bird and brush with the reserved fat. Add 1 cup (8 fl oz/250 ml) of the stock to the roasting pan.

4. Roast for 30 minutes. Reduce the oven to 375°F (190°C). Baste the bird with the cider glaze and add the remaining 1 cup (8 fl oz/250 ml) stock to the pan. Continue to roast, basting with the glaze every 15 minutes, until the juices run clear when a thigh joint is pierced or an instant-read thermometer inserted into the thickest part of the thigh away from the bone registers 180°F (82°C), about 1 hour longer. Transfer the chicken to a cutting board. Remove the onion-garlic mixture and reserve, then tent the bird with aluminum foil.

5. Place the roasting pan on the stove top over medium-high heat. Add the wine and the onion-garlic mixture, bring to a boil, and deglaze the pan, stirring to remove any browned bits from the pan bottom. Boil until reduced by half, about 10 minutes. Skim off any fat, stir in the herbs, and season with salt and pepper. Pour into a warmed serving bowl.

6. Carve the chicken at the table and pass the sauce separately.

SERVES 4-6

NUTRITIONAL ANALYSIS PER SERVING
Calories 891 (Kilojoules 3,742); Protein 60 g; Carbohydrates 55 g; Total Fat 48 g;
Saturated Fat 14 g; Cholesterol 197 mg; Sodium 616 mg; Dietary Fiber 3 g

Shrimp Brochettes with Cheese Grits

Here is a melding of ingredients and techniques that reflects the diversity of Southern cooking. The practice of grilling seafood over hardwood made its way north from the Caribbean, the spice mix is a traditional Louisiana dry rub for meats, and the creamy grits are a Dixie favorite.

1. In a bowl, combine the chili powder, garlic powder, onion powder, celery seeds, salt, and pepper. Whisk in the butter, lemon juice, Worcestershire sauce, and Tabasco. Add the shrimp and toss to coat. Cover and refrigerate for at least 1 hour or as long as overnight.

2. Meanwhile, make the grits: In a saucepan, combine the stock and milk and bring to a boil over high heat. Slowly whisk in the grits. Reduce the heat to very low, cover, and cook until thickened, about 40 minutes. Stir in the butter and season with salt and pepper. Add the cheeses, a little at a time, stirring until they melt.

3. Prepare a medium-hot fire in a grill. If using wooden skewers, soak 12 skewers in water to cover for 15 minutes.

4. About 10 minutes before the grits are ready, thread the shrimp, cherry tomatoes, and onion wedges alternately onto the skewers, piercing each shrimp twice, once in the upper back and again near the tail. Place on the grill rack about 6 inches (15 cm) from the fire and grill, turning once, until the shrimp are opaque throughout, 5–6 minutes total.

5. Divide the grits evenly among individual plates. Remove the shrimp and vegetables from the skewers, toss with the mint, and spoon over the grits. Serve immediately.

SERVES 6

NUTRITIONAL ANALYSIS PER SERVING
Calories 526 (Kilojoules 2,209); Protein 38 g; Carbohydrates 39 g; Total Fat 25 g; Saturated Fat 14 g; Cholesterol 248 mg; Sodium 852 mg; Dietary Fiber 4 g

1 tablespoon chili powder

1 teaspoon garlic powder

1 teaspoon onion powder

½ teaspoon celery seeds

½ teaspoon salt

½ teaspoon freshly ground pepper

½ cup (4 oz/125 g) unsalted butter, melted and cooled

⅓ cup (3 fl oz/80 ml) fresh lemon juice

1 tablespoon Worcestershire sauce

2 teaspoons Tabasco or other hot-pepper sauce

2 lb (1 kg) large shrimp (prawns), peeled and deveined

1 pint (12 oz/375 g) cherry tomatoes

1 large Vidalia onion, cut into 8 wedges and separated into segments

2 tablespoons chopped fresh mint

GRITS

1½ cups (12 fl oz/375 ml) chicken stock

1½ cups (12 fl oz/375 ml) milk

1 cup (6 oz/185 g) stone-ground grits

3 tablespoons unsalted butter

salt and freshly ground pepper to taste

½ cup (2 oz/60 g) shredded sharp cheddar or Swiss cheese

½ cup (2 oz/60 g) grated Parmesan cheese

Baked Snapper with Melon-Mango Salsa

SALSA

¼ honeydew melon (about 1 lb/500 g), seeded, peeled, and cut into ½-inch (12-mm) dice

2 mangoes (about ¾ lb/375 g each), pitted, peeled, and cut into ½-inch (12-mm) dice

3 kiwifruits (about ¼ lb/125 g each), peeled and cut into ½-inch (12-mm) dice

1 red (Spanish) onion, finely chopped

2 green (spring) onions, white and tender green parts only, chopped

3 cloves garlic, finely chopped

2 jalapeño chiles, seeded and finely chopped

½ cup (¾ oz/20 g) chopped fresh cilantro (fresh coriander)

¼ cup (2 fl oz/60 ml) fresh lime juice

salt and freshly ground pepper to taste

1 red snapper, 3–3½ lb (1.5–1.75 kg), cleaned with head and tail intact

4 carrots, peeled and quartered lengthwise

1 Vidalia or other sweet onion, sliced

3 tablespoons olive oil

salt and freshly ground pepper to taste

1 lemon, sliced

1 lime, sliced

a few sprigs fresh dill

1½ cups (12 fl oz/375 ml) dry white wine

The sweet and spicy salsa, inspired by the kitchens of both south Florida and Cuba, pairs beautifully with the delicate flavor of a roasted whole red snapper. Do not be intimidated by the thought of roasting a whole fish. It is much simpler than you might imagine and makes a stunning presentation.

1. To make the salsa, in a large bowl, toss together the honeydew, mangoes, kiwifruits, red onion, green onions, garlic, chiles, cilantro, lime juice, salt, and pepper. Cover and let stand at room temperature for at least 4 hours to blend the flavors, or refrigerate for up to 1 day.

2. Preheat the oven to 400°F (200°C). Select a baking dish large enough to accommodate the fish. Lightly coat the dish with vegetable oil.

3. To prepare the fish, rinse and pat dry. Using kitchen shears, snip away the fins. Layer the carrots in the prepared baking dish and top them with the onion slices. Lay the fish on top and brush the cavity and the surface with the olive oil. Season generously inside and out with salt and pepper. Cut 1 lemon slice into quarters and set aside. Arrange the remaining lemon slices and all the lime slices inside the cavity of the fish, overlapping them. Place the dill on top of the citrus slices and sew the cavity closed with a trussing kneedle and kitchen string. Pour the wine around the fish.

4. Measure the thickest part of the stuffed fish; plan on 8 minutes roasting for each 1 inch (2.5 cm) of thickness. Roast until the flesh is opaque at the bone when tested with a knife or fork, about 20 minutes. Remove from the oven and let stand for 10 minutes. With kitchen shears, carefully snip and remove the kitchen string.

5. Transfer the fish to a large platter. Surround with the salsa and garnish with the reserved lemon slice. To serve, cut along the gill line and down the backbone, carefully lifting the flesh from the bone, then turn and repeat on the other side.

SERVES 4

NUTRITIONAL ANALYSIS PER SERVING
Calories 533 (Kilojoules 2,239); Protein 45 g; Carbohydrates 64 g; Total Fat 14 g; Saturated Fat 2 g; Cholesterol 71 mg; Sodium 182 mg; Dietary Fiber 9 g

Pulled Pork with Mint Julep Barbecue Sauce

1 bone-in pork shoulder, 5 lb (2.5 kg)

2 teaspoons red pepper flakes

1 tablespoon salt

1 tablespoon freshly ground pepper

1 tablespoon yellow mustard seeds

1 cup (8 fl oz/250 ml) apple cider

1 cup (8 fl oz/250 ml) cider vinegar

4 yellow onions, thinly sliced

4 cloves garlic, chopped

1 green bell pepper (capsicum), seeded and finely chopped

12 sesame seed–topped sandwich buns, split and warmed

12 dill pickle spears

SAUCE

¼ cup (2 oz/60 g) unsalted butter

3 yellow onions, thinly sliced

2 tablespoons peeled and chopped fresh ginger

2 cups (16 fl oz/500 ml) tomato purée

¾ cup (9 oz/280 g) dark molasses

⅓ cup (3 oz/90 g) coarse-grain Dijon mustard

½ cup (4 fl oz/125 ml) bourbon

½ cup (4 fl oz/125 ml) cider vinegar

2 tablespoons Worcestershire sauce

1 lemon, sliced

salt and freshly ground pepper to taste

⅓ cup (½ oz/15 g) chopped fresh mint

1 teaspoon Tabasco or other hot-pepper sauce

In the Carolinas, barbecue sauce is a subject of fierce debate. East Carolinians prefer a spicy vinegar-based blend, West Carolinians swear by a slightly sweet tomato-based sauce, and South Carolinians favor mustard-based mixes. I have combined them all and then added a bit of bourbon and fresh mint.

1. Preheat the oven to 300°F (150°C). Lightly coat a large baking pan with vegetable oil. Rub the pork shoulder with the pepper flakes, salt, pepper, and mustard seeds and place in the baking pan. Pour the cider and vinegar over and around the pork. Scatter the onions, garlic, and bell pepper over and around the pork. Cover with aluminum foil.

2. Roast for 3 hours. Uncover and continue to roast until an instant-read thermometer inserted into the thickest part of the pork registers 180°F (82°C), about 1 hour.

3. While the pork is roasting, make the sauce: In a saucepan over medium heat, melt the butter. Add the onions and ginger and sauté until soft, about 5 minutes. Stir in the tomato purée, molasses, mustard, bourbon, vinegar, Worcestershire, lemon, salt, and pepper. Reduce the heat to very low and simmer uncovered, stirring occasionally, until very thick, about 2 hours. Discard the lemon slices. Stir in the mint and Tabasco.

4. Remove the pork from the oven and transfer to a plate. Let stand for 1 hour. Reserve the roasted vegetables. Using 2 forks, shred the pork by steadying the meat with 1 fork and pulling it away with the other, discarding any fat. Place the shredded pork in a bowl. With a slotted spoon, transfer the roasted vegetables to the bowl with the pork.

5. Mix the sauce with the shredded pork. Stuff each bun with some of the pork and serve immediately, with the pickle spears on the side.

MAKES 12 SANDWICHES

NUTRITIONAL ANALYSIS PER SANDWICH
Calories 602 (Kilojoules 2,528); Protein 30 g; Carbohydrates 55 g; Total Fat 29 g; Saturated Fat 11 g; Cholesterol 114 mg; Sodium 1,494 mg; Dietary Fiber 4 g

Southern
Barbecue

A barbecue in the South can be as grand and glorious as the famous one described on the eve of the Civil War in Margaret Mitchell's *Gone with the Wind* or as simple as a couple of friends grilling baby back ribs over ash-gray charcoal at the beach on a hot Fourth of July. In the South, the term *barbecue* refers to a piece of meat that has been slowly cooked over a fire, thereby acquiring a characteristic smoky taste. This food has been a passion of Southerners ever since Native Americans taught the first settlers how to roast wild game over a hardwood fire.

The meat is usually pork, although chicken, beef, especially in Texas, and even lamb can make their way into the barbecue pit. Traditionally, a dry seasoning mixture, called a rub, is smeared over the meat. It contains whatever the cook prefers, most often salt, pepper, sugar, and dried herbs and spices.

The fuel for the fire is a personal choice as well, ranging from hickory, oak, and pecan along the eastern seaboard and in the central South to mesquite in Texas. In parts of Florida, palmettos and corncobs are used to create the smoky heat. It is not unusual for grill masters to spend ten to twelve hours tending the flame the night before a big spread. For them, barbecuing is an art, and their sauce and rub recipes, as well as their cooking techniques, are well-guarded secrets.

Ask ten different cooks about their sauces and you will get ten different answers (that is, if they tell you anything at all). Sauces can contain molasses, bourbon, Vidalia onions, peaches, soy sauce, garlic, wine, beer, honey, mustard, allspice, cinnamon, and cloves. In fact, not much is left out of the basic sauce mixture of vinegar, tomatoes, and sweet and savory spices. The mix varies wildly by region, too. In eastern North Carolina, the sauce is thin, clear, and spicy hot, with vinegar as the base. It is usually served as a side to pulled pork shoulder and not used for basting the meat. Unsauced pulled pork is also a specialty of South Carolina's Low Country.

In western North Carolina, barbecue sauces are usually based on ketchup and are served with coleslaw over the meat. The farther north you go, the more likely the sauce is made with fresh tomatoes. In Alabama and in parts of central North Carolina,

a mustard based sauce is favored. In the western Kentucky town of Owensboro, barbecued mutton is the meat of choice and a heavy Worcestershire-laced sauce known as a black dip is served on the side.

Pork shoulder is popular in Memphis, Tennessee, but pork ribs are what the city is famous for. Dry ribs, seasoned with a dry rub, then cooked over a smoking flame, are the local specialty.

At left, a jar of home-made barbecue sauce with mop, the preferred tool for application. Below, sauce ingredients at the ready.

Game Hens with Turnip Green Stuffing

2 tablespoons unsalted butter,
   at room temperature

4 Cornish hens, 1¼ lb (625 g) each

salt and freshly ground pepper
   to taste

1 cup (8 fl oz/250 ml) apple cider

STUFFING

6 slices bacon, coarsely chopped

2 leeks, white and light green parts
   only, chopped (about 1 cup/3 oz/
   90 g)

2 cloves garlic, chopped

1 celery stalk, chopped

1 Granny Smith apple, cored and grated

½ cup (2 oz/60 g) chopped pecans

1 package (10 oz/315 g) frozen
   chopped turnip greens, thawed
   and squeezed dry

2 cups (8 oz/250 g) crumbled day-old
   corn bread

¼ cup (⅓ oz/10 g) chopped fresh
   parsley

1 tablespoon chopped fresh sage

dash of freshly grated nutmeg

salt and freshly ground pepper
   to taste

1 egg, lightly beaten

1½ cups (12 fl oz/375 ml) chicken
   stock

These stuffed hens are equally suitable for a celebratory dinner or a casual gathering.

1. Preheat the oven to 400°F (200°C). Lightly coat a roasting pan with vegetable oil. Rub the butter over the hens and season with salt and pepper. Place, breast side up, in the pan.

2. To make the stuffing, in a large frying pan over medium-high heat, cook the bacon until it begins to render some fat, about 2 minutes. Reduce the heat to medium and add the leeks, garlic, celery, apple, and pecans. Cook, stirring often, until the vegetables are soft and the nuts are aromatic, about 10 minutes. Remove from the heat and stir in the turnip greens, corn bread, parsley, sage, nutmeg, salt, pepper, egg, and chicken stock. Toss to mix well. Let stand for 10 minutes.

3. Loosely fill the cavities of each hen, including the flap of skin at the neck, with the stuffing. Truss the legs with kitchen string and tuck the wing tips beneath the breasts. Pour the apple cider around the hens. Spoon any remaining stuffing into a small buttered baking dish. Cover the roasting pan and baking dish with aluminum foil.

4. Roast the hens for 45 minutes. Uncover and continue to roast until the skin is crisped and golden brown and the juices run clear when a thigh joint is pierced, or an instant-read thermometer inserted into a breast registers 170°F (77°C), about 30 minutes longer. Slip the small baking dish in the oven for the last 30 minutes. Bake, covered, for 20 minutes, then remove the foil and bake for 10 minutes longer. Remove the hens from the oven and let stand for 15 minutes before serving.

5. Snip the strings and transfer the Cornish hens to a warmed serving platter. Serve immediately with the additional dish of stuffing.

SERVES 4

NUTRITIONAL ANALYSIS PER SERVING
Calories 1,271 (Kilojoules 5,084); Protein 67 g; Carbohydrates 55 g; Total Fat 87 g;
Saturated Fat 26 g; Cholesterol 438 mg; Sodium 1,250 mg; Dietary Fiber 7 g

Chicken with Herbed Dumplings

6 chicken breast halves, about 10 oz (315 g) each

3 qt (3 l) water

1 yellow onion, quartered

1 large carrot, quartered

1 celery stalk, quartered

1 bay leaf

1 teaspoon peppercorns

1 teaspoon salt

1 fresh parsley sprig, plus 2 table-spoons chopped

1 fresh sage sprig

1 fresh thyme sprig

1 fresh rosemary sprig

3 eggs

DUMPLINGS

3 cups (12 oz/375 g) soft winter-wheat flour, such as White Lily brand, or cake (soft-wheat) flour

½ teaspoon baking soda (bicarbonate of soda)

½ teaspoon salt

6 tablespoons (3 oz/90 g) solid vegetable shortening, chilled

⅔ cup (5 fl oz/160 ml) buttermilk

1 tablespoon fresh thyme leaves

1. In a large pot, combine the chicken breasts, water, onion, carrot, celery, bay leaf, peppercorns, and salt. Tie together the parsley sprig, sage, thyme, and rosemary sprigs and add to the pot. Bring to a boil, reduce the heat to low, and cook gently for 1 hour, skimming away any scum.

2. Remove the chicken from the pot. When cool enough to handle, remove the meat from the bones and shred it; cover and refrigerate. Return the skin and bones to the pot and simmer for 1 hour longer, adding the eggs in their shells the last 12 minutes to hard-boil them. Lift out the eggs and plunge them into an ice-water bath to stop the cooking, then peel, cover, and refrigerate until serving. Strain the stock, refrigerate until the fat rises to the surface, then lift off and discard the fat. Ladle out ⅓ cup (3 fl oz/80 ml) of the stock to use for making the dumplings; refrigerate until needed.

3. To make the dumplings, in a large bowl, sift together the flour, baking soda, and salt. Using a pastry blender or 2 knives, cut the shortening into the flour mixture until it resembles coarse meal. Make a well in the center and add the buttermilk, the ⅓ cup (3 fl oz/80 ml) stock, and the thyme. Stir to make a stiff dough. Transfer to a floured work surface and knead gently until no longer sticky, about 10 times. Pat into a round, wrap in plastic wrap, and refrigerate for at least 1 hour or as long as overnight.

4. In a saucepan over medium heat, reheat the stock. Meanwhile, on a lightly floured surface, roll out the dough about ⅛ inch (3 mm) thick. Cut into 1-by-4-inch (2.5-by-10-cm) strips. Add the strips, a few at a time, to the simmering stock. When all the dough has been added, stir gently and cook until the dumplings are firm yet tender, about 12 minutes. Add the shredded chicken and heat through, about 2 minutes longer. Adjust the seasonings.

5. Chop the reserved eggs. Ladle the chicken and dumplings into a tureen. Top with the eggs and chopped parsley and serve.

SERVES 6

NUTRITIONAL ANALYSIS PER SERVING
Calories 658 (Kilojoules 2,764); Protein 53 g; Carbohydrates 56 g; Total Fat 23 g; Saturated Fat 6 g; Cholesterol 222 mg; Sodium 514 mg; Dietary Fiber 2 g

Pork Loin with Hot-Pepper Jelly Glaze

No self-respecting Southern cook would ever be without a jar or two of hot-pepper jelly in the pantry. The contradictory sweet and spicy flavors go with everything from biscuits to roasted pork, poultry, or lamb. Look for the jelly in well-stocked specialty-foods stores.

1. Preheat the oven to 400°F (200°C). Line a large baking pan with aluminum foil. Lightly coat with vegetable oil.

2. Remove the string from the pork loin. Place the pork loin in the prepared pan and rub it with the salt and pepper. Roast for 15 minutes.

3. Reduce the oven to 350°F (180°C). Spoon the hot-pepper jelly over the pork, then spread evenly over the meat. Pour the apple cider around the pork. Return to the oven and roast, basting with the pan drippings every 10 minutes or so, until an instant-read thermometer inserted into the thickest part of the pork registers 145°F (63°C), about 45 minutes. Remove from the oven and let stand for 15 minutes before slicing.

4. Slice the pork and overlap the slices on a large warmed platter. Drizzle with the pan drippings. Garnish the platter with the Lady apples and jalapeño chiles.

SERVES 8

NUTRITIONAL ANALYSIS PER SERVING
Calories 411 (Kilojoules 1,726); Protein 49 g; Carbohydrates 22 g; Total Fat 13 g; Saturated Fat 4 g; Cholesterol 134 mg; Sodium 411 mg, Dietary Fiber 0 g

1 boneless pork loin, about 4 lb (2 kg), trimmed of visible fat and tied

1 teaspoon salt

1 tablespoon freshly cracked pepper

1 cup (10 oz/315 g) hot-pepper jelly

⅔ cup (5 fl oz/160 ml) apple cider

5 Lady apples, left whole

3 jalapeño chiles, left whole

Pecan Catfish with Banana Pepper Sauce

SAUCE

1 cup (4 oz/125 g) pecan halves, plus extra for garnish

1 cup (8 fl oz/250 ml) mayonnaise

1 shallot, chopped

1 banana chile, seeded and finely chopped

2 tablespoons chopped sweet pickle relish

2 tablespoons chopped fresh dill

juice of 1 lemon

salt and freshly ground pepper to taste

6 catfish fillets, about 6 oz (185 g) each

1 cup (8 fl oz/250 ml) buttermilk

2 eggs

1 teaspoon Tabasco or other hot-pepper sauce

½ cup (2½ oz/75 g) all-purpose (plain) flour

1 cup (5 oz/155 g) yellow cornmeal

salt and freshly ground pepper to taste

peanut oil for deep-frying

lemon wedges

Mississippi is the catfish capital of the world, raising more of this low-fat, firm-textured whitefish than any other place. Here, typical Southern ingredients—buttermilk, cornmeal, pecans, and banana peppers—complement the fish.

1. To make the sauce, preheat the oven to 400°F (200°C). Spread the pecans on a baking sheet and toast, stirring occasionally, until lightly browned and aromatic, about 8 minutes. Transfer to a plate and let cool.

2. In a food processor, pulse 1 cup (4 oz/125 g) of the cooled pecans just until they resemble a coarse meal. Do not overprocess. Remove all but ¼ cup (1 oz/30 g) of the pecan meal and set aside. Add the mayonnaise, shallot, banana chile, pickle relish, dill, lemon juice, salt, and pepper to the food processor. Pulse until well blended but still somewhat chunky. Transfer to a serving bowl, cover, and refrigerate until serving.

3. Line a baking sheet with parchment (baking) paper. Rinse the fish fillets and pat dry with paper towels. In a shallow bowl, whisk together the buttermilk, eggs, and Tabasco. In a separate shallow bowl, stir together the flour, cornmeal, reserved pecan meal, salt, and pepper. Dip each fillet into the buttermilk mixture, then coat evenly with the cornmeal mixture, shaking off any excess. Set aside on the lined baking sheet.

4. Pour peanut oil to a depth of 1 inch (2.5 cm) into a large, heavy frying pan and heat to about 360°F (180°C) on a deep-frying thermometer. Working in batches if necessary, fry the fillets, turning once, until golden brown and opaque throughout, about 3 minutes on each side. Using a slotted spatula, transfer to paper towels to drain. Keep warm until all the fillets are cooked.

5. Transfer to warmed individual plates. Garnish with lemon wedges and pecan halves. Pass the chilled sauce at the table.

SERVES 6

NUTRITIONAL ANALYSIS PER SERVING
Calories 869 (Kilojoules 3,650); Protein 34 g; Carbohydrates 37 g; Total Fat 65 g; Saturated Fat 10 g; Cholesterol 150 mg; Sodium 372 mg; Dietary Fiber 3 g

Grilled Chicken with Vidalia Onion Marmalade

MARMALADE

⅓ cup (3 fl oz/80 ml) olive oil

6 Vidalia or other sweet onions, thinly sliced

6 cloves garlic, chopped

⅔ cup (2½ oz/75 g) chopped pecans

½ cup (4 fl oz/125 ml) chicken stock

¼ cup (2 fl oz/60 ml) balsamic vinegar

1 tablespoon bourbon

¼ cup (3 oz/90 g) honey

½ cup (2 oz/60 g) grated Parmesan cheese

3 tablespoons chopped fresh rosemary

salt and freshly ground pepper to taste

6 boneless chicken breast halves with skin intact, about 6 oz (185 g) each

⅓ cup (4 oz/125 g) dark molasses

⅓ cup (3 fl oz/80 ml) fresh lime juice

2 green (spring) onions, white and tender green parts only, chopped

2 serrano chiles, sliced

2 cloves garlic, chopped

1 tablespoon peeled and chopped fresh ginger

2 tablespoons coriander seeds, lightly crushed

grated zest of 2 limes, plus lime wedges for garnish

fresh rosemary sprigs

With a little advance planning, this dish can be the stellar main course for a midsummer gathering of friends and family. Make the marmalade and marinate the chicken the evening before. Stir any leftover onion marmalade into creamy grits or mashed potatoes.

1. To make the marmalade, in a large frying pan over medium heat, warm the olive oil. Add the Vidalia onions, garlic, and pecans and cook, stirring occasionally, until the mixture begins to caramelize and turn a deep mahogany brown, about 30 minutes. Stir in the chicken stock, vinegar, and bourbon and cook until the liquid evaporates, about 10 minutes. Remove from the heat and stir in the honey, Parmesan cheese, rosemary, salt, and pepper. Set aside. (The marmalade can be covered and refrigerated for up to 1 week.)

2. Rinse the chicken breasts and pat dry. Arrange in a shallow baking dish. In a small bowl, combine the molasses, lime juice, green onions, chiles, garlic, ginger, coriander seeds, and lime zest. Pour evenly over the chicken breasts, cover, and refrigerate for 6 hours or as long as overnight.

3. Prepare a medium-hot fire in a grill.

4. Place the chicken breasts, skin side down, on the grill rack about 6 inches (15 cm) from the fire. Grill, turning once and basting frequently with the marinade, until the meat is opaque throughout and the juices run clear, about 10 minutes on each side. (Stop basting at least 5 minutes before removing the breasts from the grill.) Transfer to a cutting board and cut each breast on the diagonal into 4 or 5 slices.

5. Garnish with the lime wedges and rosemary sprigs and serve immediately with the onion marmalade.

SERVES 6

NUTRITIONAL ANALYSIS PER SERVING
Calories 705 (Kilojoules 2,961); Protein 46 g; Carbohydrates 62 g; Total Fat 33 g; Saturated Fat 7 g; Cholesterol 105 mg; Sodium 392 mg; Dietary Fiber 7 g

Country Ham with Redeye Gravy

¼ cup (2 oz/60 g) unsalted butter

4 slices country ham, each about
    4 inches (10 cm) wide, 8 inches
    (20 cm) long, and ¼ inch
    (6 mm) thick

1 cup (8 fl oz/250 ml) brewed strong
    black coffee

Redeye gravy, made from ham drippings and coffee, is a Southern standard. The country ham heats quickly, so be careful to avoid overcooking. Serve for breakfast with creamy grits and hot biscuits.

1. In a large, well-seasoned cast-iron frying pan over low heat, warm the butter, swirling it in the pan until fully melted.

2. Partially slit the country ham slices with a knife to prevent them from curling. Lay the ham slices in the pan with the fatty edges on the bottom and touching in the center and the leaner edges draped over the rim. Fry slowly until the fatty edges begin to brown, about 5 minutes. Carefully turn over the ham and cook until the fatty edges brown on the second side, about 3 minutes longer. Crowd the ham into the frying pan and cook the centers of the slices, turning once, until just heated, about 2 minutes on each side. Do not overcook, or the ham will dry out and become hard.

3. Add the brewed coffee, raise the heat to high, and bring to a boil. Boil until the liquid is reduced by three-fourths and has nicely glazed the ham, 10 minutes.

4. Transfer to warmed individual plates and serve immediately.

SERVES 4

NUTRITIONAL ANALYSIS PER SERVING
Calories 379 (Kilojoules 1,592); Protein 40 g; Carbohydrates 1 g; Total Fat 23 g;
Saturated Fat 11 g; Cholesterol 130 mg; Sodium 3,823 mg; Dietary Fiber 0 g

One of the most distinctive of all Southern delicacies is salt-cured country ham. It originated in the days before refrigeration and is now produced from corn-fed hogs in Georgia, Tennessee, Kentucky, and parts of North Carolina. The most famous of all the country hams, however, is made from peanut-fed hogs in Virginia. Called Smithfield ham, after a small town of the same name, its patented production—first salted, then smoked, then aged—is restricted by law to the city limits.

But these special hams are not the only pork in the Southern diet. Indeed, in the decades following the Civil War through the Great Depression, luxury meats were largely absent from Southern tables, replaced by vegetables seasoned with various parts of the hog, mostly the fatty sections. Nothing was wasted. To this day, Southern cooks praise the unique taste that pork fat can add to a dish. Among the many seasoning cuts found in local markets are:

Country **Ham**

Bacon Smoke-cured side pork (the meat covering the animal's spare ribs).

Fatback Salted fat containing no lean meat, from the back of the pig.

Ham Hock The lower portion of the hind leg, usually about 3 inches (7.5 cm) long, sold smoked.

Lard Rendered pork fat ideal for making flaky pie crusts and biscuits. Leaf lard is best.

Salt Pork Salt-cured side pork; usually fattier than bacon.

Streak o' Lean Similar to bacon but less meaty; usually smoked and streaked with lean meat.

Sautéed Duck Breasts with Wilted Greens

¼ cup (2 oz/60 g) unsalted butter

4 boneless duck breast halves with skin intact, 6–7 oz (185–220 g) each

salt and freshly ground pepper to taste

⅓ cup (3 fl oz/80 ml) fresh lime juice

1 tablespoon seedless blackberry preserves or honey

1 lb (500 g) dandelion greens, arugula (rocket), watercress, or baby spinach, tough stems removed

⅔ cup (2½ oz/75 g) blackberries or blueberries

2 green (spring) onions, white and pale green parts only, chopped

In the past, wild game played an integral role in Southern cooking. Today, domesticated or farm-raised game makes old-style dishes accessible to nearly everyone. These duck breasts should still be rosy pink in the center when done.

1. In a large frying pan, preferably cast iron, melt the butter over medium-high heat. Season the duck breasts with salt and pepper and place, skin side down, in the frying pan. Reduce the heat to medium and fry, turning once, until medium-rare when cut into with a knife, 3–4 minutes on each side. Transfer the duck breasts from the pan to a cutting board, crisp skin side up, and tent with aluminum foil to keep warm.

2. Return the pan to medium heat, add the lime juice, and deglaze the pan, stirring to scrape up any browned bits from the pan bottom. Add the blackberry preserves or honey and stir until melted and smooth. Add the dandelion or other greens and toss with the pan sauce until barely wilted, about 1 minute. Adjust the seasonings with salt and pepper.

3. Divide the greens among individual plates. Cut each duck breast crosswise on the diagonal into 4 or 5 slices. Fan the slices, skin side up, over the greens. Drizzle any remaining pan sauce over the duck and top with the blackberries or blueberries and green onions. Serve immediately.

SERVES 4

NUTRITIONAL ANALYSIS PER SERVING
Calories 916 (Kilojoules 3,847); Protein 24 g; Carbohydrates 16 g; Total Fat 85 g; Saturated Fat 32 g; Cholesterol 171 mg; Sodium 190 mg; Dietary Fiber 5 g

Beef with Bourbon and Mushroom Sauce

4 filets mignons, each about 6 oz (185 g) and 1¼ inches (3 cm) thick

1 teaspoon salt

2 tablespoons freshly cracked pepper

¼ cup (2 oz/60 g) unsalted butter

2 tablespoons olive oil

2 cloves garlic, chopped

2 green (spring) onions, white and tender green parts only, chopped

1½ cups (4½ oz/140 g) sliced fresh cremini mushrooms

1½ cups (12 fl oz/375 ml) beef stock

2 tablespoons bourbon

⅓ cup (3 fl oz/80 ml) heavy (double) cream

1 tablespoon Dijon mustard

Very nourishing, very sustaining, this dish comes together in less than a half hour and is delicious served with Garlic Mashed New Potatoes (page 104) or Sweet Potato–Corn Pones (page 89). A hearty Merlot will round out the flavorful meal, followed by a nap on a creaky front-porch swing.

1. Sprinkle both sides of the filets mignons with the salt and pepper and press into the meat.

2. In a large frying pan over medium-high heat, melt the butter with the olive oil. Add the steaks and cook for 2 minutes. Reduce the heat to medium, turn, and cook for 2 minutes longer. Continue cooking, turning the steaks every 2 minutes, until the desired degree of doneness is reached, about 6 minutes total for rare, 8 minutes total for medium-rare, and 10 minutes total for well done. Transfer the steaks to a platter and tent with aluminum foil to keep warm.

3. Add the garlic, green onions, mushrooms, and beef stock to the frying pan, bring to a boil over high heat, and deglaze the pan, stirring to remove any browned bits from the pan bottom. Boil until reduced by half, about 5 minutes. Stir in the bourbon and cook for 2 minutes. Add the cream and cook for 1 minute. Stir in the mustard and any accumulated juices from the cooked steaks. Taste and adjust the seasonings.

4. Spoon the warm mushroom sauce over the steaks. Serve at once.

SERVES 4

NUTRITIONAL ANALYSIS PER SERVING
Calories 760 (Kilojoules 3,192); Protein 33 g; Carbohydrates 6 g; Total Fat 65 g; Saturated Fat 29 g; Cholesterol 180 mg; Sodium 1,075 mg; Dietary Fiber 1 g

Cajun-Style Meat Loaf

Much of the cuisine in the new South is simply old-fashioned comfort food made with the freshest ingredients available. Andouille sausage gives this dish a Cajun flavor.

1. To make the sauce, in a saucepan over medium-high heat, warm the olive oil. Stir in the onion and cook until it begins to wilt, about 5 minutes. Reduce the heat to medium, stir in the flour, and cook, stirring, for 2 minutes. Add the chicken stock, wine, tomatoes, rosemary, sugar, salt, and pepper. Simmer uncovered, stirring occasionally to prevent sticking, until dark and thickened, about 30 minutes.

2. Meanwhile, preheat the oven to 400°F (200°C). Lightly coat a baking dish with vegetable oil.

3. To make the meat loaf, remove the sausages from their casings, crumble them, and place in a large bowl. Add the beef, pork, onion, garlic, celery, green olives, rolled oats, eggs, milk, basil, salt, and pepper. Mix well. Shape the mixture into a large oval and place in the prepared baking dish.

4. Bake for 30 minutes. Remove from the oven and drain off and discard any fat that has accumulated. Pour the hot tomato sauce over the meat loaf. Return to the oven and bake until the juices run clear when pierced with a knife, or an instant-read thermometer inserted into the center of the loaf registers 170°F (77°C), about 30 minutes longer. Remove from the oven and let rest, uncovered, for 15 minutes.

5. Transfer the meat loaf to a warmed platter and slice to serve.

SERVES 8

NUTRITIONAL ANALYSIS PER SERVING
Calories 677 (Kilojoules 2,843); Protein 33 g; Carbohydrates 27 g; Total Fat 48 g; Saturated Fat 17 g; Cholesterol 167 mg; Sodium 909 mg; Dietary Fiber 4 g

SAUCE

1 tablespoon olive oil

1 Vidalia or other sweet onion, chopped

1 tablespoon all-purpose (plain) flour

½ cup (4 fl oz/125 ml) chicken stock

½ cup (4 fl oz/125 ml) dry red wine

1 can (1 lb/500 g) crushed tomatoes with added purée

1 tablespoon chopped fresh rosemary

2 teaspoons sugar

salt and freshly ground pepper to taste

MEAT LOAF

1 lb (500 g) andouille sausage

1 lb (500 g) lean ground (minced) beef

1 lb (500 g) lean ground (minced) pork

1 Vidalia or other sweet onion, finely chopped

4 cloves garlic, finely chopped

1 celery stalk, chopped

½ cup (2½ oz/75 g) sliced pimiento-stuffed green olives

½ cup (1½ oz/45 g) rolled oats

2 eggs, lightly beaten

¼ cup (2 fl oz/60 ml) milk

2 tablespoons chopped fresh basil

salt and freshly ground black pepper to taste

Peach-and-Bourbon-Basted Pork Chops

3 tablespoons yellow or brown
   mustard seeds

⅓ cup (3 fl oz/80 ml) fresh lemon
   juice

1 cup (10 oz/315 g) peach preserves

½ cup (4 fl oz/125 ml) mayonnaise

⅓ cup (3 oz/90 g) Dijon mustard

¼ cup (2 fl oz/60 ml) bourbon

2 shallots, finely chopped

1 tablespoon chopped fresh rosemary

salt and freshly ground pepper
   to taste

6 pork loin chops, each 6 oz (185 g)
   and about ¾ inch (2 cm) thick

½ cup (2 oz/60 g) dried bread crumbs

This quick, tasty dish is the perfect choice for a make-ahead dinner. Coat the pork chops with the glaze the night before and store, tightly covered, in the refrigerator. When you are ready to cook them, sprinkle on the bread crumbs and place in the preheated oven. You'll need to add about 10 minutes to the cooking time if the chops are still quite cold.

1. Preheat the oven to 400°F (200°C). Lightly butter a large baking dish.

2. In a bowl, combine the mustard seeds and lemon juice. Let stand for 30 minutes. Add the peach preserves, mayonnaise, mustard, bourbon, shallots, rosemary, salt, and pepper. Spread about one-third of the glaze on the bottom of the prepared baking dish. Arrange the pork chops on top of the glaze. Evenly spread the remaining glaze over the chops. Sprinkle with the bread crumbs.

3. Bake until just a hint of pink remains in the pork, about 35 minutes. Transfer to warmed individual plates and serve immediately.

SERVES 6

NUTRITIONAL ANALYSIS PER SERVING
Calories 675 (Kilojoules 2,835); Protein 26 g; Carbohydrates 41 g; Total Fat 44 g; Saturated Fat 12 g; Cholesterol 105 mg; Sodium 613 mg; Dietary Fiber 2 g

Creole Vegetables with Crawfish Tails

2 ears of yellow or white corn, husks and silk removed

⅓ cup (3 fl oz/80 ml) bacon drippings or peanut oil

⅓ cup (2 oz/60 g) all-purpose (plain) flour

2 yellow onions, chopped

2 celery stalks, chopped

2 green bell peppers (capsicums), seeded and chopped

4 cloves garlic, chopped

1 or 2 finger hot, bird's eye, or jalapeño chiles, seeded and finely chopped

2 cups (16 fl oz/500 ml) chicken stock

1 can (28 oz/875 g) crushed tomatoes with added purée

1 lb (500 g) baby lima beans, shelled

1 lb (500 g) small okra, sliced

1 lb (500 g) fresh or thawed frozen crawfish tails or small shrimp (prawns), peeled and deveined

3 green (spring) onions, chopped

salt and freshly ground pepper to taste

filé powder for dusting

RICE

2 cups (14 oz/440 g) long-grain white rice

4½ cups (36 fl oz/1.1 l) chicken stock or water

2 tablespoons unsalted butter

salt and freshly ground pepper to taste

The Creoles were the original French and Spanish colonists of New Orleans. The Cajuns were French immigrants from Acadia (now known as Nova Scotia) who subsequently settled on the bayous of the Louisiana swamp country. This basic gumbo combines the cooking styles and ingredients of both heritages.

1. Resting an ear of corn on its stalk end in a shallow bowl, cut down along the ear with a sharp knife, stripping off the kernels and rotating the ear with each cut. Then run the flat side of the blade along the ear to remove any "milk." Repeat with the remaining ear. Set aside.

2. In a large, heavy saucepan over medium heat, warm the bacon drippings or peanut oil. Stir in the flour and cook, stirring constantly, until the mixture (called a roux) is a dark caramel color, about 20 minutes. Do not allow it to burn, or the dish will have a scorched taste.

3. Stir in the onions, celery, bell peppers, garlic, and chiles and cook, stirring occasionally, until the vegetables are soft, about 10 minutes. Add the stock, tomatoes, corn, lima beans, and okra and cook uncovered, stirring often, until slightly thickened, about 40 minutes.

4. Meanwhile, cook the rice: In a large saucepan over medium-high heat, combine the rice, chicken stock or water, butter, salt, and pepper. Bring to a boil, reduce the heat to low, cover, and simmer until the rice is tender, about 20 minutes. Remove from the heat and let stand, covered, for about 10 minutes. Fluff with a fork. Taste and adjust the seasonings.

5. Add the crawfish tails or shrimp and the green onions to the vegetable mixture and cook over medium heat until the shellfish is cooked through and turns coral pink, about 5 minutes. Season with salt and pepper.

6. Spoon the rice onto individual plates. Ladle the vegetables and seafood over the rice. Dust each serving with filé powder and serve at once.

SERVES 6

NUTRITIONAL ANALYSIS PER SERVING
Calories 706 (Kilojoules 2,965); Protein 29 g; Carbohydrates 110 g; Total Fat 17 g; Saturated Fat 6 g; Cholesterol 95 mg; Sodium 1,450 mg; Dietary Fiber 12 g

A roux is a flavorful mixture of a flour and a fat, sometimes oil, sometimes butter, sometimes lard. It is the base of a gravy or sauce and is also used to thicken such Louisiana dishes as gumbo (see Creole Vegetables with Crawfish Tails, opposite) and étouffée.

The best vessel to use for making a roux is a heavy pot or cast-iron frying pan. The usual ratio of flour to fat is one to one (by volume). Depending upon the desired color, a roux can take anywhere from two minutes (a blond roux) up to an hour (a black roux, most often used in gumbos). Generally, blond and medium roux are used in gravies and sauces.

Although all gravies are sauces, not all sauces are gravies. A gravy is a sauce made from meat juices, usually combined with broth, milk, or cream and thickened with a roux or other thickener. Most Southerners love a good gravy. Indeed, most of us consider it a beverage. Anyone who is unfamiliar with the milk or cream gravy served throughout the South might question our passion for this concoction, but it plays an important role in the cuisine, marrying fried chicken with rice, sausage

Gravy, Sauce, and **Roux**

with biscuits, and roast beef with mashed potatoes.

Like a gravy, a sauce is a thickened liquid used to accompany and highlight the flavor of foods. But the similarity stops there. Sauces can be made not only from meat juices, but also from simmered vegetables, puréed fruits, or such sweet sources as chocolate or caramel.

Southern Seafood Country Captain

2 tablespoons unsalted butter

2 tablespoons olive oil

2 yellow onions, thinly sliced

2 carrots, peeled and shredded

1 each green, red, and yellow bell
  pepper (capsicum), seeded and
  thinly sliced

4 cloves garlic, chopped

2 tablespoons mild curry powder,
  preferably Madras

1 cup (8 fl oz/250 ml) dry white wine

1 can (1 lb/500 g) diced tomatoes
  with juice

1 can (28 oz/875 g) crushed tomatoes
  with added purée

1 tablespoon chopped fresh sage

1 teaspoon sugar

salt and freshly ground pepper
  to taste

1 lb (500 g) shrimp (prawns), peeled
  and deveined

½ lb (250 g) bay scallops

½ lb (250 g) fresh-cooked lump
  crabmeat, picked over for shell
  fragments

1 lb (500 g) catfish fillets, cut into
  1-inch (2.5-cm) nuggets

FOR SERVING

about 6 cups (2 lb/1 kg) hot cooked
  white rice

toasted almonds, golden raisins
  (sultanas), grated orange zest,
  chopped green (spring) onions,
  mango chutney

I have adapted a traditional Southern chicken dish, transforming it into an elegant and easy-to-serve seafood creation in which the flavors of India are paired with the elements of down-home cuisine. Serve over white rice with a simple green salad, crusty bread, and ice-cold beer.

1. To prepare the seafood sauce, in a large, heavy saucepan over medium heat, melt the butter with the olive oil. Add the yellow onions, carrots, bell peppers, garlic, and curry powder. Stir well and cook, stirring, until the onions and peppers begin to wilt and the curry powder is fragrant, about 5 minutes. Add the white wine, bring to a boil, and cook until the liquid has almost evaporated, about 10 minutes. Stir in the diced tomatoes, crushed tomatoes, sage, sugar, salt, and pepper. Reduce the heat to low and simmer uncovered, stirring occasionally, until the sauce is thick and lustrous, about 40 minutes.

2. Remove the sauce from the heat and stir in the shrimp, scallops, crabmeat, and catfish. Cover and allow the seafood to cook in the hot sauce until the shrimp are pink and curled and the scallops and catfish are opaque throughout, about 10 minutes. Taste and adjust the seasonings.

3. Spoon the hot rice onto a large serving platter or individual plates. Ladle the seafood sauce liberally over the rice. Garnish with the almonds, raisins, orange zest, and green onions. Serve at once. Pass the mango chutney at the table.

SERVES 6

NUTRITIONAL ANALYSIS PER SERVING
Calories 786 (Kilojoules 3,301); Protein 49 g; Carbohydrates 89 g; Total Fat 26 g;
Saturated Fat 8 g; Cholesterol 190 mg; Sodium 1,387 mg; Dietary Fiber 6 g

3 Breads & Sides

To paraphrase Tennessee Williams, the South has always depended on the kindness of nature. Sunny days, ample rain, a long growing season, short, cool nights, and good soil have long made the South an agricultural Mecca, with the result that breads and side dishes have always played an important role in the local diet. For decades after the Civil War, the South struggled, and the Southern table, rich with grains and vegetables and short on meat, reflected the hard times. Those days have not been forgotten: go to any authentic Southern diner today, order the blue-plate special, and you'll get "a meat and three"—one main course, and all of three side dishes.

Sour Cream and Chive Spoon Bread

2 cups (16 fl oz/500 ml) milk

½ cup (4 fl oz/125 ml) water

2 tablespoons unsalted butter

1 teaspoon salt

½ teaspoon freshly ground pepper

1 cup (5 oz/155 g) yellow cornmeal

⅔ cup (5 fl oz/160 ml) sour cream

4 eggs

1½ cups (6 oz/185 g) shredded
cheddar cheese

⅓ cup (½ oz/15 g) chopped fresh
chives

A question has vexed Southerners for generations: "Is spoon bread a bread or a side dish?" Let's just say it is a winning combination of both. Spoon bread resembles a grits casserole, but it has a lighter, softer, more custardy texture and is made with cornmeal. It is delicious served alongside country ham or fried chicken.

1. Preheat the oven to 350°F (180°C). Lightly butter a 1½-qt (1.5-l) soufflé dish.

2. In a saucepan over medium-high heat, combine the milk, water, butter, salt, and pepper. Bring to a boil over high heat and slowly whisk in the cornmeal. When the mixture returns to a boil, reduce the heat to medium and continue whisking until the mixture thickens and pulls away from the sides of the pan, about 3 minutes. Remove from the heat and whisk in the sour cream.

3. In a bowl, using a handheld electric mixer set at high speed, beat the eggs until thick and a pale lemon yellow, about 5 minutes. Gradually stir about one-fourth of the hot cornmeal mixture into the beaten eggs, then fold the eggs into the remaining cornmeal mixture, stirring constantly. Fold in the cheese and chives. Pour into the prepared soufflé dish.

4. Bake until a toothpick inserted into the center comes out clean, about 35 minutes. Serve at once.

SERVES 6

NUTRITIONAL ANALYSIS PER SERVING
Calories 396 (Kilojoules 1,663); Protein 17 g; Carbohydrates 24 g; Total Fat 26 g; Saturated Fat 15 g; Cholesterol 206 mg; Sodium 661 mg; Dietary Fiber 1 g

Braised Cabbage with Tasso

HOT-PEPPER VINEGAR
4–6 fresh chiles such as jalapeño or
  serrano, split lengthwise

4–6 dried chiles, broken in half
  crosswise

1 fresh rosemary sprig

2 cups (16 fl oz/500 ml) cider vinegar

½ large head green cabbage, cored

½ large head red cabbage, cored

¼ cup (2 oz/60 g) unsalted butter

¼ lb (125 g) tasso, coarsely chopped

3 yellow onions, chopped

2 celery stalks, chopped

1 green bell pepper (capsicum), seeded
  and chopped

4 green (spring) onions, white and
  tender green parts only, chopped

4 cloves garlic, chopped

½ cup (4 fl oz/125 ml) chicken stock

salt and freshly ground pepper
  to taste

Tasso, a Cajun specialty, is lean, cured pork shoulder or beef highly seasoned with cayenne pepper, garlic, and filé powder and then smoked. Thick-cut country bacon or country ham can be substituted here, although the unique flavor of tasso will be missing. If you don't have time to let your homemade hot-pepper vinegar mellow for a month, store-bought will do just fine.

1. To make the vinegar, place the fresh and dried chiles and rosemary sprig in a sterilized 3-cup (24–fl oz/750-ml) bottle with a tight-fitting cork. In a saucepan over medium-high heat, bring the vinegar to a boil. Remove from the heat and pour into the bottle. Let cool, cork the bottle, and place in a cool, dark place. Let stand for 1 month, gently shaking the bottle every 2 or 3 days, before using. Once opened, store in the refrigerator for up to 6 months.

2. Chop each cabbage half into about 8 pieces. In a large saucepan over medium heat, melt the butter. Add the tasso, onions, celery, bell pepper, green onions, and garlic. Cook, stirring often, until the vegetables just begin to wilt, about 10 minutes. Add the cabbage and continue to cook, stirring occasionally, until the cabbage leaves are wilted and separated, about 10 minutes. Add the chicken stock, cover, reduce the heat to very low, and cook, stirring occasionally, until the cabbage is very tender, about 1 hour.

3. Season with salt and pepper and transfer to a bowl. Serve hot or at room temperature. Pass the hot-pepper vinegar at the table.

SERVES 8

NUTRITIONAL ANALYSIS PER SERVING
Calories 158 (Kilojoules 664); Protein 8 g; Carbohydrates 18 g; Total Fat 8 g;
Saturated Fat 4 g; Cholesterol 25 mg; Sodium 484 mg; Dietary Fiber 5 g

W hen Southerners speak of greens, they are talking about the edible leaves of certain plants such as collard, mustard, beet, turnip, and dandelion. Greens have played an important role in the South's culinary heritage, in large part because some of them grew wild and were foraged when the larder was low.

Collard greens, a hearty wintertime member of the cabbage family, typically are slowly cooked in water seasoned with salt pork, which helps to tame the greens' assertive, bitter flavor. This creates an additional treat known as pot likker, the leftover cooking broth that is often served as a soup. Turnip greens carry the same tonic bitterness as their collard kin, and are traditionally served for good luck on New Year's Day. Dark green, peppery mustard greens rank second only to collard greens in popularity in Southern cooking.

Beet greens, the leafy tops of the common garden beet, should be removed as soon as possible after purchase or pulling, as they draw moisture from the beet root. The spinach or leaf beet, commonly known as Swiss chard or chard, is also popular in the South. So, too,

Peppery, Leafy **Greens**

are dandelion greens, which grow wild in meadows and are widely cultivated as well. Try the slightly bitter leaves raw in salads or quickly cooked like spinach.

Other greens in the Southern larder include watercress, poke salet, and lamb's quarters. Some are cultivated. Some grow wild. All have a delicious peppery bite.

Sally Lunn Herbed Rolls

5 teaspoons (2 packages) active dry yeast

⅓ cup (3 oz/90 g) sugar

1 cup (8 fl oz/250 ml) warm milk (110°F/43°C)

4 eggs

2 teaspoons salt

4 cups (1¼ lb/625 g) bread (hard-wheat) flour

½ cup (4 oz/125 g) unsalted butter, melted

½ cup (¾ oz/20 g) mixed chopped fresh herbs such as parsley, sage, rosemary, and thyme

1 egg beaten with 1 tablespoon milk

18 fresh flat-leaf (Italian) parsley or sage leaves

The French *soleil, lune,* "sun, moon," provides the name for this old English recipe because the top of each roll bakes up as golden as the sun, while the bottom is said to be as pale as a harvest moon. Sally Lunn rolls have been a part of Southern heritage for so long, we claim them as our own.

1. In a small bowl, combine the yeast, sugar, and milk. Let stand until frothy, about 10 minutes.

2. In the bowl of a stand mixer fitted with the paddle attachment, beat together the eggs and salt until fluffy and a pale lemon yellow, about 5 minutes. Add the yeast mixture and beat until smooth, about 1 minute. Add the flour to the egg mixture in three batches alternately with the melted butter, beginning and ending with the flour. Beat in the chopped herbs. Cover with plastic wrap and let rise in a warm place until doubled in volume, about 2 hours.

3. Preheat the oven to 350°F (180°C). Lightly butter 18 standard muffin cups.

4. Punch down the dough with a wooden spoon. Scoop out and divide the batter among the prepared muffin cups. Lightly butter a sheet of plastic wrap and place, buttered side down, over the muffins. Let rise again until doubled in volume, about 45 minutes.

5. Uncover the rolls and lightly brush the tops with the egg-milk mixture. Lay 1 whole herb leaf on the center of each roll. Bake until a toothpick inserted into the center of a roll comes out clean, about 25 minutes. Transfer to a wire rack and let cool for 5 minutes. Turn out of the pan onto the rack and let cool completely before serving.

MAKES 18 ROLLS

NUTRITIONAL ANALYSIS PER ROLL
Calories 219 (Kilojoules 920); Protein 6 g; Carbohydrates 29 g; Total Fat 8 g; Saturated Fat 5 g; Cholesterol 77 mg; Sodium 296 mg; Dietary Fiber 1 g

Grits and Black-Eyed Pea Fritters

SAUCE

¾ cup (6 fl oz/180 ml) mayonnaise

2 tablespoons fresh lemon juice

2 tablespoons prepared horseradish

2 teaspoons Dijon mustard

1 teaspoon Worcestershire sauce

2 tablespoons capers

1 tablespoon chopped fresh flat-leaf
   (Italian) parsley

salt and freshly ground pepper to taste

3 cups (24 fl oz/750 ml) water

3 tablespoons unsalted butter

salt to taste, plus 1 teaspoon

freshly ground pepper to taste, plus
   ½ teaspoon

¾ cup (4½ oz/140 g) quick-cooking
   grits

6 slices bacon, chopped

1½ cups (10½ oz/330 g) drained,
   cooked black-eyed peas *(page 98)*,
   slightly mashed

2 eggs, lightly beaten

4 green (spring) onions, including
   tender green tops, minced

1 or 2 chipotle chiles, soaked in boiling
   water for 30 minutes, then drained,
   seeded, and minced

2 cloves garlic, minced

1 teaspoon ground cumin

3 tablespoons peanut oil

2 tablespoons chopped fresh flat-leaf
   (Italian) parsley

1. To make the sauce, in a small bowl, whisk together the mayonnaise, lemon juice, horseradish, mustard, Worcestershire sauce, capers, and parsley. Season with salt and pepper. Cover and refrigerate until serving.

2. Line a 9-by-5-inch (23-by-13-cm) loaf pan with plastic wrap, leaving enough overhanging the sides to cover the top later.

3. In a saucepan, combine the water, butter, and salt and pepper to taste and bring to a boil over high heat. Slowly whisk in the grits, then reduce the heat to medium. Simmer, whisking occasionally, until the grits are bubbly and thickened, about 5 minutes. Transfer to a bowl and let cool slightly.

4. In a frying pan over medium-high heat, fry the bacon until crisp, about 5 minutes. Using a slotted spoon, transfer to paper towels to drain briefly, then add to the grits along with the black-eyed peas, eggs, green onions, chiles, garlic, cumin, the 1 teaspoon salt, and the ½ teaspoon pepper. Mix well. Spoon into the prepared loaf pan, smoothing the top. Cover with the overhanging plastic wrap and press gently to remove any air pockets. Refrigerate until firm, several hours or as long as overnight.

5. Carefully invert the loaf pan onto a cutting board, lift off the pan, and peel away the plastic wrap. Cut the loaf into 12 equal slices. Cut each slice on the diagonal, forming 24 triangles in all.

6. In a large frying pan over medium-high heat, warm the peanut oil until it sizzles. Reduce the heat to medium. Add the triangles in batches and cook, turning once, until lightly browned and heated through, about 5 minutes total. Using tongs, transfer to a warmed platter and keep warm.

7. Arrange the fritters on a serving platter and sprinkle with the parsley. Pass the sauce at the table.

MAKES 24 FRITTERS; SERVES 8

NUTRITIONAL ANALYSIS PER FRITTER
Calories 126 (Kilojoules 529); Protein 2 g; Carbohydrates 8 g; Total Fat 10 g;
Saturated Fat 2 g; Cholesterol 18 mg; Sodium 211 mg; Dietary Fiber 2 g

Corn
The Amazing Grain

C orn, native to the Western Hemisphere, is a paragon of versatility, a fact that puts it at the center of every Southern cook's pantry. It is eaten straight off the cob and is turned into cornmeal, hominy, grits, corn oil, corn syrup, cornstarch (cornflour), and bourbon.

Southerners grow both yellow and white corn varieties. Yellow corn has larger, fuller-flavored kernels, while white corn has smaller, sweeter ones. It is best to use corn as soon as possible after picking, as its sugars immediately begin to turn to starch, reducing the natural sweetness and toughening the kernels.

The corn introduced to the early colonists by Chief Powhatan and the Algonquin Indians is not the same as the corn we grow today. Native Americans usually dried the kernels, which they called hominy, and often combined them with dried beans to make the original succotash, a dish that contemporary cooks commonly prepare with fresh corn and beans and sometimes a little salt pork. Today, the production of hominy involves boiling corn kernels in a lye solution, then hulling, washing, and drying them.

One of the most common side dishes on the Southern table is hominy grits, most often simply called grits, a soft, savory cornmeal mush made from ground yellow or white hominy. Grits, which are sold in different grinds and can be stone-ground or steel-ground, are usually slowly simmered in water, milk, or cream, although a quick-cooking version also is sold. Long a down-home specialty, they now appear on more upscale menus thanks to the addition of various ingredients such as cheeses and herbs.

Cornmeal is ground from dried corn kernels, and may be white or yellow, depending on the color of the corn. Available in a variety of grinds and either stone- or steel-ground, it is used for many Southern breads, including corn bread; corn pone; corn muffins; hush puppies; hoecakes, sometimes called Johnny cakes; and spoon bread.

Finally, there is bourbon, the only corn-based distilled spirit to originate in the United States. It began in the mountains of Bourbon County, Kentucky, as a primitive corn whiskey called moonshine or the more rough-and-tumble white lightning. By the 1800s, distillers had discovered that shipments in wooden casks developed a smoother, mellower spirit. This led

to storing the amber liquid in leak-proof barrels made from charred wood to improve the taste and character. Today, bourbon is a connoisseur's delight, a straight (unblended) corn whiskey that, according to law, must be made with a minimum of 51 percent corn, with wheat or rye and barley malt making up the balance. Southerners use this celebrated spirit in everything from mint juleps (see page 136) to barbecue sauces to apple pies.

Grits, cornmeal, cornstarch, and hominy (left) are all at home in the kitchen. Stone-ground grits (below) with melting butter.

Grits and Greens Soufflé

½ lb (250 g) mixed assorted greens such as turnip, collard, mustard, or Swiss chard, tough stems removed

¼ cup (2 oz/60 g) unsalted butter

½ Vidalia or other sweet onion, chopped

1 clove garlic, chopped

¼ cup (2 fl oz/60 ml) chicken stock

1¾ cups (14 fl oz/430 ml) milk

½ cup (4 fl oz/125 ml) heavy (double) cream

¾ cup (4½ oz/140 g) quick-cooking grits

3 green (spring) onions, white and pale green parts only, chopped

1½ teaspoons fresh thyme leaves

salt and freshly ground pepper to taste

½ cup (2 oz/60 g) shredded cheddar cheese

3 eggs, separated

½ cup (2 oz/60 g) grated Parmesan cheese

Grits and greens pair naturally in the South, like red Georgia clay on a five-year-old's knees or sticky fingers and ice cream at a church social. This soufflé will not rise as tall as a traditional one, but it will still puff up and lighten in texture.

1. Preheat the oven to 350°F (180°C). Lightly butter a 9-by-13-inch (23-by-33-cm) baking or gratin dish.

2. Stack 5 or 6 leaves of the greens on top of one another and roll up tightly. Cut on a diagonal into thin strips. Repeat with the remaining greens.

3. In a large frying pan over medium-high heat, melt the butter. Add the greens, sweet onion, and garlic and cook, stirring occasionally, until the greens are wilted, about 10 minutes. Add the stock, reduce the heat to medium, cover partially, and cook until the greens are tender, about 20 minutes longer. Remove from the heat and let cool. Pour into a sieve and drain well, pressing out any excess liquid. Transfer to a large bowl. Reserve the cooking liquid for another use.

4. In a saucepan over medium heat, combine the milk and cream and bring to a simmer. Slowly whisk in the grits, green onions, thyme leaves, salt, and pepper. Cook, stirring frequently to prevent the grits from sticking, until thick and creamy, about 5 minutes. Remove from the heat and stir in the cheddar cheese. Add to the greens and stir to combine well.

5. In a small bowl, lightly beat the egg yolks with a fork, then quickly stir into the grits mixture. In a large bowl, using an electric mixer set on high speed, beat the egg whites until stiff peaks form. Stir one-fourth of the egg whites into the grits mixture to lighten it, then, using a rubber spatula, gently fold the lightened grits into the remaining egg whites. Pour the mixture into the prepared dish. Top with the Parmesan cheese.

6. Bake until puffed and golden, about 40 minutes. Serve at once.

SERVES 6

NUTRITIONAL ANALYSIS PER SERVING
Calories 401 (Kilojoules 1,684); Protein 15 g; Carbohydrates 26 g; Total Fat 27 g;
Saturated Fat 16 g; Cholesterol 183 mg; Sodium 369 mg; Dietary Fiber 2 g

Carolina Rice Pilaf

¼ cup (2 oz/60 g) unsalted butter

1 yellow onion, chopped

2 celery stalks, chopped

6 oz (185 g) fresh button mushrooms, sliced

1 carrot, peeled and shredded

2½ cups (17½ oz/545 g) long-grain white rice

6½ cups (52 fl oz/1.6 l) chicken or beef stock

salt and freshly ground black pepper to taste

6 oz (185 g) chopped assorted dried fruits such as apples, pears, apricots, and dates

½ teaspoon red pepper flakes

4 green (spring) onions, including tender green tops, chopped

½ cup (2½ oz/75 g) slivered blanched almonds, lightly toasted

Although the days of rice being a major crop in South Carolina have passed, the grain remains a constant on dinner tables throughout the state. It turns up in everything from salads to seafood stews to puddings. Pilaf, in countless guises, is arguably its most celebrated preparation. Here, a mixture of dried fruits imparts sweetness to this pantry staple.

1. In a large saucepan over medium-high heat, melt the butter until it just begins to brown. Stir in the onion, celery, mushrooms, and carrot and cook, stirring occasionally, until fragrant, about 5 minutes. Stir in the rice and cook, stirring, until well coated, about 3 minutes longer. Stir in the stock, salt, and black pepper. Bring to a boil, reduce the heat to low, cover, and cook until the liquid has been absorbed, about 20 minutes.

2. Remove from the heat. Stir in the dried fruit, red pepper flakes, green onions, and almonds. Cover and let stand for 10 minutes. Fluff with a fork and adjust the seasonings with salt and black pepper. Serve at once.

SERVES 8

NUTRITIONAL ANALYSIS PER SERVING
Calories 427 (Kilojoules 1,793); Protein 9 g; Carbohydrates 71 g; Total Fat 13 g; Saturated Fat 5 g; Cholesterol 16 mg; Sodium 836 mg; Dietary Fiber 4 g

Sweet Potato–Corn Pones

Corn pones are shaped and baked corn bread dumplings. In some parts of the South, mashed sweet potatoes are added to the batter for a more tender crumb and a slightly sweeter flavor. Serve warm with butter to accompany country ham or fried catfish. Heat any leftovers for breakfast and drizzle them with honey, sorghum, or cane syrup.

1. Preheat the oven to 400°F (200°C). Pierce the sweet potatoes several times with a fork and place directly on the center rack of the oven. Bake until very soft when pierced, about 50 minutes. Transfer to a cutting board, cut in half lengthwise, and let cool for 5 minutes.

2. Brush a well-seasoned ovenproof griddle with vegetable oil. Reduce the oven temperature to 350°F (180°C) and place the griddle in the oven.

3. Scoop the potato flesh from its skins into a bowl. Add the melted butter or other fat and mash while still warm. In a separate bowl, stir together the cornmeal, brown sugar, salt, baking soda, and nutmeg. Add the cornmeal mixture to the sweet potatoes. Stir in the egg and just enough buttermilk to make a stiff batter. Be careful not to overmix.

4. Remove the griddle from the oven. With 2 spoons, form the batter into small ovals about the size of an egg. Place on the hot griddle and flatten slightly. Return the griddle to the oven and bake until the pones are puffed and golden brown, about 30 minutes. Serve warm.

MAKES ABOUT 16 PONES

NUTRITIONAL ANALYSIS PER PONE
Calories 133 (Kilojoules 559); Protein 3 g; Carbohydrates 24 g; Total Fat 3 g;
Saturated Fat 1 g; Cholesterol 17 mg; Sodium 201 mg; Dietary Fiber 2 g

about 2 lb (1 kg) sweet potatoes

2 tablespoons melted unsalted butter, vegetable oil, or bacon drippings

2 cups (10 oz/315 g) yellow cornmeal, preferably stone-ground

1 tablespoon light brown sugar

1 teaspoon salt

½ teaspoon baking soda (bicarbonate of soda)

freshly grated nutmeg to taste

1 egg, lightly beaten

about ½ cup (4 fl oz/125 ml) buttermilk

Minted Green Snap Beans

2 lb (1 kg) green beans, strings and
ends removed

1 red (Spanish) onion, thinly sliced

1 red bell pepper (capsicum), seeded
and cut lengthwise into strips
¼ inch (6 mm) wide

¼ cup (2 fl oz/60 ml) raspberry
vinegar

1 tablespoon whole-grain Dijon
mustard

1 teaspoon sugar

salt and freshly ground pepper
to taste

¼ cup (2 fl oz/60 ml) extra-virgin
olive oil

½ cup (¾ oz/20 g) chopped fresh
mint

Green beans are sometimes called snap beans because of
the sound garden-fresh beans make when broken in half.
They are known as string beans, too, for the long fibrous
thread that traditionally runs the length of the pod.

1. Bring a large saucepan three-fourths full of salted water to a boil. Add
the green beans and cook until just crisp-tender, about 3 minutes. Drain
and rinse under cold running water to stop the cooking. Drain again.

2. In a large serving bowl, toss together the green beans, red onion,
and bell pepper.

3. In a small bowl, whisk together the vinegar, mustard, sugar, salt,
and pepper. Slowly whisk in the olive oil until thick and emulsified. Add
half of the mint and mix well.

4. Drizzle the dressing over the vegetables and toss well. Sprinkle with
the remaining mint just before serving. Serve at room temperature.

SERVES 6

NUTRITIONAL ANALYSIS PER SERVING
Calories 144 (Kilojoules 605); Protein 3 g; Carbohydrates 14 g; Total Fat 10 g;
Saturated Fat 1 g; Cholesterol 0 mg; Sodium 72 mg; Dietary Fiber 3 g

Skillet Corn Bread with Crisp Sage Leaves

3 ears of yellow corn, husks and silk removed

¼ cup (2 fl oz/60 ml) vegetable oil

16 whole fresh sage leaves

2 cups (10 oz/315 g) ground yellow cornmeal

½ cup (2½ oz/75 g) all-purpose (plain) flour

1 tablespoon sugar

1 tablespoon baking powder

1 teaspoon salt

½ teaspoon baking soda (bicarbonate of soda)

2 cups (16 fl oz/500 ml) buttermilk

2 eggs, lightly beaten

2 tablespoons unsalted butter, melted

Corn bread in any form boasts a loyal following in the South. You can buy plain cornmeal or self-rising (leavening already added) cornmeal or a complete corn bread mix (just add water). Yellow and white cornmeal can be used interchangeably, although I prefer the slightly coarser yellow variety.

1. Resting an ear of corn on its stalk end in a shallow bowl, cut down along the ear with a sharp knife, stripping off the kernels and rotating the ear with each cut. Then run the flat side of the blade along the ear to remove any "milk." Repeat with the remaining ears. You should have about 2 cups (12 oz/375 g) kernels in all.

2. Preheat the oven to 450°F (230°C). Pour the vegetable oil into a 10-inch (25-cm) well-seasoned cast-iron frying pan and place in the oven. Heat until sizzling hot, about 5 minutes. Remove from the oven and lay the sage leaves evenly in the frying pan. Return the frying pan to the oven for 5 minutes to crisp the sage leaves.

3. Meanwhile, in a bowl, sift together the cornmeal, flour, sugar, baking powder, salt, and baking soda. Stir in the buttermilk, eggs, and butter just until mixed. Add the corn kernels and stir to blend. Do not overmix.

4. Spoon the batter over the crisp sage leaves, return to the oven, and reduce the temperature to 400°F (200°C). Bake until golden brown and a toothpick inserted into the center comes out clean, about 25 minutes. Transfer to a wire rack to cool for 5 minutes, then invert and carefully cut into 8 wedges. Serve immediately.

MAKES 8 WEDGES

NUTRITIONAL ANALYSIS PER WEDGE
Calories 326 (Kilojoules 1,369); Protein 8 g; Carbohydrates 48 g; Total Fat 12 g; Saturated Fat 3 g; Cholesterol 37 mg; Sodium 633 mg; Dietary Fiber 3 g

The cast-iron frying pan is probably the most often-used utensil in the Southern kitchen, essential to frying the crispiest chicken or baking the most delectable corn bread. Many local cooks consider these indispensable pans cherished family heirlooms, to be lovingly passed down through the generations.

Cast-iron pots and pans were in the earliest Southern kitchens, where cooks appreciated the ability of the dark, porous metal to absorb and hold heat better than most other metals. Care must be taken, however, to preserve the life of this fundamental pan. First of all, never wash it with soap, which removes the oil buildup that gives it its well-seasoned, almost nonstick character. Instead, soak it in hot water and then wipe it clean and dry with a cloth or paper towel. Lightly rub the cleaned pan with peanut or vegetable oil before putting it away.

If rust spots form, pour some salt over the discolored area and rub with a damp cloth until the spots disappear. The salt acts as a light abrasive, and you will need to reseason the pan. To do so, clean it with mild dishwashing detergent and a stiff

Cast-Iron **Frying Pan**

brush (this is the only time you should ever use soap on it), grease it inside and out with vegetable oil, place it in the center of a preheated 300°F (150°C) oven for an hour, and then turn the oven off and let the pan cool in the oven overnight. Remove any excess oil with a slightly damp cloth. Follow this same procedure to season a newly purchased pan.

Sweet Potato and Cracked Pepper Biscuits

1 large yellow sweet potato, about 10 oz (315 g)

½ cup (4 fl oz/125 ml) buttermilk

3 cups (15 oz/465 g) soft winter-wheat self-rising flour such as White Lily brand

1 tablespoon light brown sugar

1 teaspoon freshly cracked pepper

½ teaspoon salt

¼ cup (2 oz/60 g) chilled unsalted butter, cut into small cubes, plus 2 tablespoons melted

2 tablespoons solid vegetable shortening, chilled

The rite of passage from amateur Southern cook to accomplished baker is achieved with a perfect batch of biscuits. The secret to making these light, flaky breads is passed down from generation to generation.

1. Preheat the oven to 400°F (200°C). Prick the sweet potato several times with a fork and place directly on the center rack of the oven. Bake until very soft when pierced, about 1 hour. Let cool, peel, place in a bowl, and mash with a fork until very smooth. Whisk in the buttermilk.

2. Raise the oven temperature to 450°F (230°C) and preheat for at least 15 minutes. Lightly grease a large baking sheet.

3. In a bowl, combine 2 cups (10 oz/315 g) of the flour, the brown sugar, pepper, and salt. Using a pastry blender, 2 knives, or your fingers, cut in the butter cubes and shortening until the mixture resembles a coarse meal. Shake the bowl occasionally so that the larger pieces come to the top and can be worked to a consistent size, about that of peas. Make a well in the center and add the sweet potato mixture to it. Stir with a fork to moisten evenly. Do not overwork it. Sprinkle about ¼ cup (1½ oz/45 g) of the remaining flour over the top, turn the dough over, and sprinkle with another ¼ cup (1½ oz/45 g) of the flour.

4. Flour your hands well, pinch off a piece of dough about the size of an egg, dip the wet part of the dough into the remaining ½ cup (2 oz/60 g) flour, and knead gently into a ball. The dough should not be too sticky or too wet. Flatten slightly and place on the prepared baking sheet. Repeat with the remaining dough, placing the biscuits so they just barely touch. Brush the tops lightly with the melted butter.

5. Bake until golden brown, 18–20 minutes. Transfer to a wire rack and let cool for 5 minutes. Serve at once.

MAKES 12 BISCUITS

NUTRITIONAL ANALYSIS PER BISCUIT
Calories 210 (Kilojoules 882); Protein 4 g; Carbohydrates 33 g; Total Fat 7 g; Saturated Fat 3 g; Cholesterol 11 mg; Sodium 560 mg; Dietary Fiber 1 g

Collard Greens with Benne Seeds and Chile Oil

2 lb (1 kg) collard greens, mustard greens, turnip greens, or broccoli rabe, tough stems and wilted leaves discarded

2 tablespoons olive oil

6 cloves garlic, thinly sliced

2 dried hot chiles, broken in half crosswise

¼ cup (¾ oz/20 g) sesame seeds

1 tablespoon chopped fresh rosemary

2 tablespoons honey

salt and freshly ground pepper to taste

2 tablespoons cider vinegar

1 tablespoon hot chile oil

The unexpected flavors of this dish exemplify contemporary Southern cuisine at its best. The greens are not cooked for hours as in my grandmothers' day, and the toasty flavors of the benne (sesame) seeds pair nicely with the bitterness of the vegetable. If you prefer, use hot-pepper vinegar instead of the cider vinegar and chile oil.

1. Cut the greens into 1-inch (2.5-cm) pieces. Bring a large saucepan three-fourths full of lightly salted water to a boil over high heat. Add the greens and stir to immerse completely in the water. Return to a boil, reduce the temperature to medium, and cook until crisp-tender, about 10 minutes. Drain and place under cold running water to stop the cooking. Transfer to a large kitchen towel, wrap well, and squeeze out as much excess water as possible.

2. In a large frying pan with deep sides, warm the olive oil over medium heat. Add the garlic, chiles, sesame seeds, and rosemary and cook, stirring, until the sesame seeds begin to lightly brown, about 1 minute. Stir in the greens and honey. Sauté, stirring occasionally, until the greens are well coated with the other ingredients and heated through, about 3 minutes. Season with salt and pepper.

3. Transfer to a large bowl and drizzle with the vinegar and chile oil just before serving.

SERVES 6

NUTRITIONAL ANALYSIS PER SERVING
Calories 139 (Kilojoules 584); Protein 2 g; Carbohydrates 15 g; Total Fat 9 g; Saturated Fat 1 g; Cholesterol 0 mg; Sodium 19 mg; Dietary Fiber 4 g

White Acre Peas with Dried Chiles

1 smoked ham hock, about ¾ lb (375 g)

2 dried hot chiles

3 qt (3 l) water

4 cups (2 lb/1 kg) shelled White Acre peas, black-eyed peas, or lima beans (about 6 lb/3 kg unshelled)

salt and freshly ground pepper to taste

I have spent many lazy summer afternoons sitting in an old porch glider shelling White Acre peas with the rhythmic creak of the glider, the chorus of chirping crickets, and the hum of honeybees the only sounds breaking the stillness. Some of the pea pods are small and tender and can be eaten without shelling. Just break them in half before cooking.

1. In a large saucepan, combine the ham hock, chiles, and water and bring to a boil over high heat. Reduce the heat to medium and cook, uncovered, until the liquid is reduced by half, about 30 minutes.

2. Add the peas, raise the heat to high, and bring to a boil. Reduce the heat to low, cover, and simmer until the peas are tender, about 30 minutes. If the peas begin to dry out before they are cooked, add a little water. Season with salt and pepper.

3. Transfer to a warmed bowl and serve immediately.

SERVES 8

NUTRITIONAL ANALYSIS PER SERVING
Calories 184 (Kilojoules 773); Protein 13 g; Carbohydrates 29 g; Total Fat 2 g; Saturated Fat 1 g; Cholesterol 8 mg; Sodium 194 mg; Dietary Fiber 6 g

To a Southerner, the term *field pea* encompasses a whole family of peas available fresh, dried, canned, or frozen. The most famous of them is the black-eyed pea, a small, tan bean with a round, black "eye" and a pleasantly earthy flavor. The same bean is sometimes called a cowpea, and if the eye is pale rather than dark, it can also be dubbed a yellow-eyed pea. Originally, Southerners cultivated black-eyed peas for animal feed, but after the Civil War, with the region devastated, everyone from field hands to fine ladies found themselves eating them. They are the traditional ingredient in Hoppin' John Chowder (see page 25) and in the marinated mélange of peas and chopped vegetables known as Mississippi Caviar (see page 28) or, depending upon where you are from, Texas or Georgia caviar.

Another popular pea, the deep reddish brown crowder pea, has a heartier flavor than its black-eyed cousin. It is traditionally simmered with ham hocks and served with chowchow, a sharp-flavored, mustardy vegetable relish believed to have been introduced to the Southern table by Chinese railroad workers.

Field **Peas**

Two other field peas turn up in the Southern pantry. The Purple Hull pea is pale and slightly elongated, with a definite but much smaller eye and a firmer texture than the black-eyed pea. Lady peas, also known as White Acre peas, are light, either cream or ivory colored, and have no eye. They are the tiniest of the field peas and, in my opinion, the tastiest.

Yellow Squash and Corn Custard

4 ears of yellow corn, husks and silk
   removed

2 tablespoons olive oil

3 yellow summer squashes, about
   18 oz (560 g) total weight, coarsely
   chopped (about 2½ cups)

1 banana chile, halved, seeded, and
   thinly sliced

1 red bell pepper (capsicum), seeded
   and chopped

1 yellow onion, chopped

4 cloves garlic, chopped

6 egg yolks

1 cup (8 fl oz/250 ml) milk

½ cup (4 fl oz/125 ml) sour cream

1 tablespoon fresh thyme leaves

dash of freshly grated nutmeg

salt and freshly ground pepper
   to taste

1 cup (4 oz/125 g) shredded sharp
   cheddar cheese

boiling water, as needed

In summertime, my Granny Lou would work her magic turning farm-fresh corn and yellow squash into this easy casserole. I could hardly get my chores done around the farm thinking about this delicious dish waiting for me on the lunch table.

1. Preheat the oven to 375°F (190°C). Lightly coat a 2½-qt (2½-l) soufflé or baking dish with vegetable oil.

2. Working with 1 ear of corn at a time, hold by its pointed end, steadying its stalk end on a cutting board. Using a sharp knife, cut down along the ear to strip off the kernels, turning the ear with each cut. You should have about 3 cups (18 oz/560 g) kernels in all.

3. In a large frying pan over medium-high heat, warm the olive oil until it sizzles. Add the corn kernels, squashes, banana chile, bell pepper, onion, and garlic and cook, stirring occasionally, until soft, about 10 minutes. Remove from the heat.

4. In a bowl, combine the egg yolks, milk, sour cream, thyme, nutmeg, salt, and pepper. Whisk until smooth. Stir in the vegetable mixture and the cheese. Pour into the prepared dish.

5. Set the dish in a shallow pan and pour boiling water into the pan to a depth of about 2 inches (5 cm). Bake until the custard is set and a knife inserted into the center comes out clean, about 45 minutes. Let cool for 10 minutes before serving.

SERVES 8

NUTRITIONAL ANALYSIS PER SERVING
Calories 264 (Kilojoules 1,109); Protein 10 g; Carbohydrates 21 g; Total Fat 17 g;
Saturated Fat 7 g; Cholesterol 185 mg; Sodium 128 mg; Dietary Fiber 3 g

Fried Green Tomatoes with Goat Cheese

6 slices bacon, coarsely chopped

1 cup (5 oz/155 g) all-purpose (plain) flour

1 cup (5 oz/155 g) yellow cornmeal

1 teaspoon salt

1 teaspoon freshly ground pepper

4 green tomatoes, sliced ½ inch (12 mm) thick

about ½ cup (4 fl oz/120 ml) peanut oil

¼ lb (125 g) soft fresh goat cheese

1 large, very ripe tomato, seeded and finely diced

The hit movie of the same name brought this Southern side dish to national prominence a few years back. But in the frugal South, we have been enjoying fried green tomatoes for generations. With artisan cheese makers popping up all over the region, I've added a contemporary goat cheese layer to the traditional recipe.

1. In a large frying pan, preferably cast iron, fry the bacon over medium-high heat until crisp, about 5 minutes. Using a slotted spoon, transfer to paper towels to drain. Pour off about half of the drippings and discard. Reserve the bacon.

2. In a pie dish or shallow bowl, stir together the flour, cornmeal, salt, and pepper. Coat each tomato slice on both sides with the seasoned flour and place on a wire rack.

3. Add about ¼ cup (2 fl oz/60 ml) of the peanut oil to the drippings in the pan and place over medium-high heat. When hot, add the tomato slices, in batches, and cook, turning once, until golden brown and crisp, about 1 minute on each side. Using a slotted spatula, transfer to paper towels to drain. Repeat with the remaining slices, adding more peanut oil as needed.

4. Carefully spread about 1 teaspoon of the goat cheese on each slice. Arrange the tomato slices, overlapping them, on a round serving plate and top with the diced tomato and the bacon. Serve at once.

SERVES 4

NUTRITIONAL ANALYSIS PER SERVING
Calories 657 (Kilojoules 2,759); Protein 17 g; Carbohydrates 64 g; Total Fat 37 g; Saturated Fat 12 g; Cholesterol 28 mg; Sodium 902 mg; Dietary Fiber 4 g

Garlic Mashed New Potatoes

3½ lb (1.75 kg) small new potatoes,
  unpeeled

12 cloves garlic, peeled

1 celery stalk, coarsely chopped

¼ cup (2 oz/60 g) unsalted butter,
  at room temperature

1 cup (8 fl oz/250 ml) heavy
  (double) cream

salt and freshly ground pepper
  to taste

In this down-home version of everybody's favorite side dish, the potatoes are mashed with their skins still on, along with garlic and celery, which adds flavor and produces an appealing appearance. Serve alongside Country-Fried Steak with Vidalia Onion Gravy (page 40).

1. In a large saucepan, combine the potatoes, garlic, and celery with salted water to cover. Bring to a boil over high heat, reduce the heat to low, cover, and simmer until the potatoes are very tender when pierced, about 30 minutes. Drain well and return to the pan.

2. Using a potato masher, crush the potatoes, garlic, and celery. Place over low heat, add the butter, and continue mashing until the butter melts. With a wooden spoon, stir in the cream until well incorporated and the potatoes begin to fluff up, about 1 minute.

3. Transfer to a warmed serving bowl, season with salt and pepper, and serve at once.

SERVES 8

NUTRITIONAL ANALYSIS PER SERVING
Calories 321 (Kilojoules 1,348); Protein 5 g; Carbohydrates 38 g; Total Fat 17 g;
Saturated Fat 10 g; Cholesterol 56 mg; Sodium 32 mg; Dietary Fiber 3 g

Mirlitons Stuffed with Rice and Cheese

The mirliton made its way north to Louisiana from Central and South America and the West Indies via the port of New Orleans. Because of its mild flavor, it benefits from the addition of assertive seasonings.

1. Preheat the oven to 400°F (200°C). Select a baking dish large enough to hold the mirlitons snugly and lightly coat with vegetable oil.

2. Cut each mirliton in half lengthwise. Remove and discard the seeds. Place the mirliton halves in a vegetable steamer basket set over boiling water. Cover and steam until the mirlitons are tender when pierced with a fork, about 12 minutes.

3. Drain the mirlitons and let cool. Scoop out the flesh with a melon baller or grapefruit spoon, leaving a shell about ¼ inch (6 mm) thick. Coarsely chop the flesh.

4. In a frying pan over medium-high heat, warm the olive oil. Add the rice, pecans, onion, garlic, curry powder, and mirliton flesh and cook until the onion is soft, about 5 minutes. Transfer to a bowl and let cool.

5. Stir the bread crumbs, Gruyère cheese, tomatoes, egg, basil, salt, and pepper into the mirliton mixture. Divide the mixture evenly among the mirliton halves, mounding it in the center. Place in the baking dish, with the sides touching. Sprinkle the Parmesan cheese evenly over the tops.

6. Bake until golden brown and heated through, about 20 minutes. Remove from the oven and let stand for 10 minutes before serving.

7. Drizzle each squash with a splash of cider vinegar, if desired, and serve at once.

SERVES 8

NUTRITIONAL ANALYSIS PER SERVING
Calories 275 (Kilojoules 1,155); Protein 11 g; Carbohydrates 21 g; Total Fat 17 g;
Saturated Fat 5 g; Cholesterol 47 mg; Sodium 201 mg; Dietary Fiber 2 g

4 mirlitons, about ½ lb (250 g) each

3 tablespoons olive oil

1 cup (5 oz/155 g) cooked long-grain white rice

½ cup (2 oz/60 g) chopped pecans

1 red (Spanish) onion, chopped

2 cloves garlic, chopped

1 teaspoon hot curry powder, preferably Madras

1 cup (2 oz/60 g) fresh bread crumbs

1 cup (4 oz/125 g) shredded Gruyère cheese

3 ripe tomatoes, seeded and chopped

1 egg, lightly beaten

3 tablespoons chopped fresh basil

salt and freshly ground pepper to taste

⅓ cup (1½ oz/45 g) grated Parmesan cheese

cider vinegar for drizzling (optional)

Angel-Light Beignets

⅔ cup (5 fl oz/160 ml) warm water (115°F/46°C)

¼ cup (2 oz/60 g) granulated sugar

¼ teaspoon salt

2½ teaspoons (1 package) active dry yeast

3½–4 cups (17½–20 oz/545–625 g) all-purpose (plain) flour

⅓ cup (3 fl oz/80 ml) heavy (double) cream

1 egg, lightly beaten

peanut oil for deep-frying

confectioners' (icing) sugar for dusting

Beignets (pronounced "ben-YAYS") are a traditional New Orleans deep-fried yeast pastry. In the heart of the French Quarter at the Café du Monde, every good day starts and often ends with a plate of these airy golden treats and a cup of chicory-infused café au lait.

1. In a 2-cup (16–fl oz/500-ml) measuring cup, combine the water, granulated sugar, salt, and yeast. Let stand until frothy, about 10 minutes.

2. Measure out 3½ cups (17½ oz/545 g) of the flour into a food processor. With the processor motor running, slowly add the yeast mixture, processing until fully absorbed. Add the cream and egg and process to form a soft dough. Add more flour, 1 tablespoon at a time, until the dough cleans the sides of the work bowl and is no longer sticky. Continue processing for 1 minute to knead. Place in a lightly oiled lock-top plastic bag, seal, and refrigerate overnight.

3. Transfer the dough to a lightly floured work surface and punch it down to eliminate air pockets. Using a floured rolling pin, roll out the dough into an 8-inch (20-cm) square about ¾ inch (2 cm) thick. With a sharp knife, square off the corners. Cut the dough into sixteen 2-inch (5-cm) squares, then cut the squares in half on the diagonal to form 32 triangles. Transfer to a lightly floured baking sheet and let rise, uncovered, until doubled in size, about 45 minutes.

4. Pour peanut oil to a depth of 4 inches (10 cm) into a heavy saucepan and heat to 375°F (190°C) on a deep-frying thermometer. Add the pieces of dough, a few at a time, and deep-fry, turning as needed, until golden, about 1 minute. Using a slotted spoon, transfer to paper towels to drain.

5. Sprinkle generously with confectioners' sugar and serve hot.

MAKES 32 BEIGNETS

NUTRITIONAL ANALYSIS PER BEIGNET
Calories 108 (Kilojoules 454); Protein 2 g; Carbohydrates 16 g; Total Fat 4 g;
Saturated Fat 1 g; Cholesterol 10 mg; Sodium 21 mg; Dietary Fiber 1 g

Old Town
PRALINE SHO[P]
627 ROYAL ST.
Our Pralines Are Made Fresh Dail[y]
In our own kitchen in courtyard
we will ship for you

4 Desserts & Drinks

Home-baked pies, cakes, cookies, puddings, and cobblers fuel the notorious Southern sweet tooth. It's no wonder that even our terms of endearment—honey, sugar, cupcake, cutie pie—revolve around the sweeter things in life. Today, most big celebrations, whether a holiday gathering, a birthday, or an anniversary, call for an extraordinary dessert, such as a coconut layer cake. Other events—a church supper, a PTA meeting, a bridge game—prompt bakers to turn out their specialties, from chess pie to Key lime squares. The South is also known for a famous drink or two. Certainly, lemonade and sweet iced tea are regional icons, not to mention the mint julep and the mojito. Recipes follow.

Old-Fashioned Vanilla Seed Pound Cake

2½ cups (10 oz/315 g) soft winter-wheat flour, such as White Lily brand, or cake (soft-wheat) flour

1¼ cups (10 oz/315 g) sugar

1 tablespoon baking powder

½ teaspoon salt

1 cup (8 oz/250 g) unsalted butter, at room temperature

⅓ cup (3 fl oz/80 ml) sour cream

5 eggs, lightly beaten

2 teaspoons vanilla extract (essence)

1 vanilla bean, split lengthwise

Pound cake, originally made with a pound (500 g) each of butter, eggs, sugar, and flour, is a long-time Southern favorite. This cake is flavored and flecked with vanilla bean seeds. The addition of sour cream provides extra moistness.

1. Preheat the oven to 325°F (165°C). Lightly butter a 10-inch (25-cm) tube pan, then coat with flour, tapping out the excess. Line the bottom of the pan with waxed paper cut to fit precisely and butter and flour the paper.

2. In a large bowl, combine the flour, sugar, baking powder, and salt. With a handheld electric mixer set on low speed, mix to combine the dry ingredients. Add the butter and sour cream with half of the beaten eggs. Increase the speed to medium and beat for 1 minute, stopping once or twice to scrape down the sides of the bowl. Add the remaining eggs and the vanilla extract. Using the tip of a knife, scrape the seeds from the vanilla bean halves into the mixture. Beat for 30 seconds longer. Pour into the prepared pan.

3. Bake until a toothpick inserted into the center comes out clean, about 1¼ hours, covering the top loosely with aluminum foil if it begins to brown too quickly. Transfer to a wire rack and let cool for 10 minutes. Gently loosen the edges of the cake with a thin-bladed knife or icing spatula, invert onto the rack, and peel away the waxed paper. Carefully turn the cake upright and let cool completely before serving.

SERVES 10

NUTRITIONAL ANALYSIS PER SERVING
Calories 440 (Kilojoules 1,848); Protein 6 g; Carbohydrates 52 g; Total Fat 23 g; Saturated Fat 14 g; Cholesterol 161 mg; Sodium 307 mg; Dietary Fiber 0 g

Peaches Foster

⅓ cup (3 fl oz/80 ml) dark rum

½ cup (3 oz/90 g) golden raisins (sultanas)

½ cup (4 oz/125 g) unsalted butter

⅔ cup (5 oz/155 g) firmly packed light brown sugar

4 large, ripe peaches, peeled, pitted, and sliced (about 3 cups/18 oz/ 560 g)

¼ teaspoon ground cinnamon

1 qt (1 l) vanilla ice cream

⅓ cup (1½ oz/45 g) sliced (flaked) almonds, lightly toasted

4 fresh mint sprigs

In 1951, a chef at the famous Brennan's in New Orleans created a flaming banana concoction as a breakfast dish in honor of one of the restaurant's faithful patrons, Mr. Richard Foster. Since then, it has become synonymous with the South. My variation uses juicy ripe peaches instead.

1. In a small bowl, pour the rum over the raisins and let stand until plump, about 30 minutes.

2. In a large frying pan over medium-high heat, melt the butter. Add the brown sugar and stir until melted and bubbly, about 2 minutes. Reduce the heat to medium and add the peaches. Cook, stirring gently so as not to break up the slices, until tender, about 3 minutes. Sprinkle with the cinnamon and stir in the raisins and rum. Heat until the rum is very fragrant, about 1 minute. Remove from the heat, carefully tilt the pan, and ignite the rum with a long match. The flames will subside in about 15 seconds.

3. Spoon the vanilla ice cream in scoops into 4 individual bowls. Ladle the peaches and rum sauce over the ice cream. Garnish each serving with the almonds and a mint sprig. Serve at once.

SERVES 4

NUTRITIONAL ANALYSIS PER SERVING
Calories 826 (Kilojoules 3,469); Protein 9 g; Carbohydrates 99 g; Total Fat 43 g; Saturated Fat 24 g; Cholesterol 120 mg; Sodium 127 mg; Dietary Fiber 4 g

Molasses Chess Pie

pastry dough *(page 124)*

4 eggs

1¼ cups (10 oz/315 g) sugar

pinch of salt

½ teaspoon vanilla extract (essence)

¼ cup (2 oz/60 g) unsalted butter, melted and cooled

¼ cup (3 oz/90 g) dark molasses

¼ cup (2 fl oz/60 ml) buttermilk or heavy (double) cream

¼ cup (2 fl oz/60 ml) fresh lemon juice

2 tablespoons yellow cornmeal

1 tablespoon finely grated lemon zest

freshly grated nutmeg for dusting

A few different accounts offer possible explanations for the name of this pie. One claims it comes from the word *chest,* as pies of the era were commonly stored in pie safes or chests. Whatever the origin, this pie is a regional classic.

1. Make the pastry dough and roll out and fold into quarters as directed. Place in a 9-inch (23-cm) pie pan, unfold, and then press gently into the bottom and sides of the pan. Trim the edges to create a 1-inch (2.5-cm) overhang and fold the overhang under itself. Press the edges with fork tines or flute attractively with your fingers. Chill in the freezer for 30 minutes.

2. Preheat the oven to 400°F (200°C). Crumple a sheet of waxed paper, then flatten it out in the pastry-lined pan, spreading it to the edges. Fill with pie weights or dried beans. Bake the pastry until very lightly browned around the edges, about 20 minutes. Transfer to a wire rack and carefully remove the weights and paper. Let cool completely. Raise the oven temperature to 450°F (230°C).

3. In a bowl, using an electric mixer set on medium speed, beat together the eggs, sugar, salt, and vanilla until thick, fluffy, and a pale lemon yellow, about 5 minutes. Add the butter, molasses, buttermilk or cream, lemon juice, cornmeal, and lemon zest and beat until well combined. Pour into the cooled crust. Lightly dust the top with nutmeg.

4. Place in the oven and immediately reduce the heat to 325°F (165°C). Bake until just set in the center, about 35 minutes. Transfer to a wire rack to cool. Serve warm or at room temperature.

SERVES 8

NUTRITIONAL ANALYSIS PER SERVING
Calories 442 (Kilojoules 1,856); Protein 5 g; Carbohydrates 59 g; Total Fat 21 g; Saturated Fat 10 g; Cholesterol 138 mg; Sodium 210 mg; Dietary Fiber 0 g

Sugarcane took root in Florida and Louisiana with the arrival of the Spanish from the West Indies in the sixteenth century. A labor-intensive crop, it flourished on plantations whose work-forces were fed by the growing African slave trade.

Although sugarcane is still grown in the southern reaches of Florida and the delta-laced parishes of Louisiana, highly mechanized equipment has replaced the hand harvesting of the past. The cane is shredded to extract its natural sweet juice, which is clarified and sent to evaporators, where most of the liquid is removed. Next it is heated to eliminate more liquid, leaving dry crystals, what we know as raw sugar. Finally, the crystals are spun at high speed, separating out what are the beginnings of molasses. What remains is sent to refineries, where it is turned into white table sugar.

Molasses is made by boiling the sugarcane liquid released from the crystals. Light molasses, the result of the first boiling, is sweet and mild, delicate enough to be used as a topping. Dark molasses, from the second boiling, is less sweet and is used in baking. Slightly bitter blackstrap

Cane **Sugar**

molasses, the product of the third boiling, is used sparingly in cooking, as its flavor can be overpowering.

Cane syrup is made by boiling sugarcane juice to the consistency of maple syrup, basically one process shy of light molasses. Although it is used primarily in baking, it is also wonderful spooned over homemade vanilla ice cream—a real treat.

Shortcakes with Berries and Crème Fraîche

2½ cups (12½ oz/390 g) soft winter-wheat self-rising flour such as White Lily brand

½ cup (2½ oz/75 g) yellow cornmeal

1 teaspoon baking soda (bicarbonate of soda)

1 teaspoon ground cinnamon

½ teaspoon salt

¼ cup (2 oz/60 g) firmly packed light brown sugar

½ cup (4 oz/125 g) plus 2 tablespoons chilled unsalted butter, cut into ½-inch (12-mm) cubes

1 cup (8 fl oz/250 ml) buttermilk

1 cup (8 fl oz/250 ml) sour cream

½ teaspoon vanilla extract (essence)

3 tablespoons milk

3 tablespoons granulated sugar mixed with ½ teaspoon ground cinnamon

1 cup (4 oz/125 g) sliced strawberries

3 cups (12 oz/375 g) mixed blackberries, raspberries, and blueberries

½ cup (4 oz/125 g) granulated sugar

2 cups (16 fl oz/500 ml) crème fraîche, sour cream, or whipped heavy (double) cream

fresh mint sprigs

Shortcake has long been a summertime favorite. This updated version is still right at home served with barbecue and lemonade on the Fourth of July.

1. Preheat the oven to 450°F (230°C). Lightly butter a large baking sheet.

2. In a bowl, sift together the flour, cornmeal, baking soda, cinnamon, and salt. Then, push the brown sugar through the sieve into the bowl with your fingers or a spoon. Using a pastry blender or 2 knives, cut in the butter until the mixture resembles a coarse meal. In a small bowl, whisk together the buttermilk, the 1 cup (8 fl oz/250 ml) sour cream, and the vanilla. Make a well in the center of the flour mixture and pour in the buttermilk mixture. Stir with a fork to moisten evenly; a wet dough will form.

3. Drop the dough by heaping spoonfuls (about ½ cup/4 oz/125 g each) into 8 equal mounds on the prepared baking sheet, spacing them about 2 inches (5 cm) apart. With floured hands, lightly shape each mound into a 3-inch (7.5-cm) round about ½ inch (12 mm) thick. Brush the tops with the milk and sprinkle with the sugar-cinnamon mixture.

4. Bake until golden brown, 15–18 minutes. Transfer to a wire rack to cool completely.

5. In a large bowl, stir together the strawberries, blackberries, raspberries, blueberries, and granulated sugar until the sugar dissolves.

6. With a serrated knife, cut the cooled shortcakes in half horizontally and place the bottoms, cut sides up, on 8 dessert plates. Place a dollop of the crème fraîche, sour cream, or whipped cream on each bottom. Top with some of the berries and crown with an additional dollop of cream. Position the top of each shortcake slightly offset from the bottom. Garnish the plates with the remaining berries and the mint. Serve at once.

SERVES 8

NUTRITIONAL ANALYSIS PER SERVING
Calories 746 (Kilojoules 3,133); Protein 10 g; Carbohydrates 77 g; Total Fat 44 g;
Saturated Fat 27 g; Cholesterol 105 mg; Sodium 962 mg; Dietary Fiber 4 g

Classic Southern Pralines

3 cups (1½ lb/750 g) sugar

3½ cups (14 oz/440 g) pecan halves

1⅓ cups (11 fl oz/345 ml) buttermilk

6 tablespoons (3 oz/90 g) unsalted
butter

¼ teaspoon salt

1 teaspoon vanilla extract (essence)

½ teaspoon almond extract (essence)

1½ teaspoons baking soda (bicarbonate of soda)

Although the idea of mixing nuts (traditionally almonds) with caramelized sugar is French in origin, these pralines are Louisiana ingenuity pure and simple. The earliest recipes called for locally grown pecans and raw sugar brought into the port of New Orleans from Cuban cane fields. Avoid making pralines on a humid day. They will not set up properly.

1. Line 2 baking sheets with waxed paper.

2. In a large, heavy saucepan over low heat, combine the sugar, pecan halves, buttermilk, butter, and salt. Cook, stirring occasionally, until the sugar dissolves completely, about 10 minutes. Do not allow the mixture to boil before the sugar dissolves or it may crystallize and become grainy. Raise the heat to medium-high and bring to a boil, stirring occasionally but being careful not to scrape any hardened candy mixture from the sides of the saucepan. Cook to the soft-ball stage, 236°–239°F (113°–115°C) on a candy thermometer, about 15 minutes.

3. Remove from the heat and stir in the vanilla and almond extracts and the baking soda. As soon as you add the baking soda, the mixture will become lighter in color and foamy in texture. Beat rapidly with a wooden spoon until the mixture begins to cool, thicken, and lose some of its shine, 5–7 minutes.

4. Working quickly, drop the candy by heaping tablespoonfuls, using one spoon to scoop and another to push the mixture onto the prepared baking sheets. Let stand at room temperature until firm, about 1 hour. Eat immediately, or store between layers of waxed paper in an airtight container for up to 10 days.

MAKES ABOUT 3 DOZEN PRALINES

NUTRITIONAL ANALYSIS PER PRALINE
Calories 168 (Kilojoules 706); Protein 1 g; Carbohydrates 21 g; Total Fat 9 g;
Saturated Fat 2 g; Cholesterol 6 mg; Sodium 78 mg; Dietary Fiber 1 g

Soft-Wheat
Flour

After the Civil War and well into the new century, young Southern women were judged by the quality of their baking. It was common practice for women "of a certain marrying age" to bake a pie or cake or batch of cookies for auctioning off at a church bazaar or community social. Male suitors would submit a secret bid on the dessert that caught their eye, and the successful bidder would win not only the dessert but also a chaperoned date with the baker. Today, although dessert-making skills are not generally considered critical in the search for the perfect partner, every good Southern baker still relies on the region's soft-wheat flour for making pies, cakes, and biscuits.

Climate and geography contribute to making the South this nation's soft winter-wheat capital. Winter wheat is grown in places where, even in the coldest months, the ground freezes to a depth of 10 inches (25 cm) or less. It's called "soft" for its relative lack of protein (between 7.5 and 9.5 percent protein), glutenin being the protein many bakers know and gliadin, its less familiar kin. When flour mixes with water, glutenin goes on to form gluten, the structure that gives dough its elasticity. Gliadin goes on to contribute softness, the quality that helps make a cake's crumb tender. Because of its well-measured makeup, soft winter-wheat flour is perfectly suited for delicate batters and tender-crumbed biscuits, rolls, and quick breads. This flour is available in bleached, self-rising (with a chemical leavener added), and whole-wheat varieties.

By contrast, hard spring wheat flourishes in colder climes, generally speaking above the Mason-Dixon Line. It's used to produce all-purpose flours that contain between 9.5 and 12 percent protein, and that lend themselves to sturdy, often yeast-risen, doughs. All-purpose flour is available in bleached, unbleached, self-rising, and whole-wheat varieties.

In the past, the majority of soft wheat in the United States was grown in Georgia, North Carolina, Virginia, Kentucky, Tennessee, and southern Ohio. Today, Indiana, Illinois, and Michigan join the list.

Since 1883, Knoxville, Tennessee, has been the home of White Lily flour, probably the best known and most available brand of Southern

milled soft winter-wheat flour. Other brands include Martha White, Gladiola, and Red Band.

If you're not able to find flour made from soft winter wheat, cake flour, fine-textured and low in protein (about 8 percent protein), makes a good substitute. In place of self-rising Southern flour, try 1 cup (4 oz/125 g) cake flour, 1½ teaspoons baking powder, ½ teaspoon baking soda, and ½ teaspoon salt for each cup of the self-rising.

Some say soft winter-wheat flour (left) is the secret to Southern baking. Orange angel food cake (below) is a crowd pleasing example of Southern baking at its best.

Key Lime Bars

2½ cups (12½ oz/390 g) all-purpose (plain) flour

½ cup (2 oz/60 g) confectioners' (icing) sugar, plus extra for dusting

½ cup (4 oz/125 g) chilled unsalted butter, cut into ½-inch (12-mm) cubes

3 oz (90 g) chilled cream cheese, cut into ½-inch (12-mm) cubes

¼ teaspoon almond extract (essence)

4 eggs

2 cups (1 lb/500 g) granulated sugar

½ cup (4 fl oz/125 ml) fresh Key lime juice (8–10 limes)

1 teaspoon vanilla extract (essence)

grated zest of 4 Key limes (about 1 tablespoon)

I always return from the Florida Keys with Key limes. I freeze the juice and zest for later use in tropical drinks, "Floribbean" cuisine, or this delectable dessert. Although the tartness of Key limes is preferred for this recipe, the more familiar Persian limes can be substituted.

1. Preheat the oven to 350°F (180°C).

2. In a food processor, combine 2¼ cups (11¼ oz/350 g) of the flour, the ½ cup (2 oz/60 g) confectioners' sugar, the butter, cream cheese, and almond extract. Pulse until the mixture is crumbly but holds together when squeezed between your fingers. Working quickly, transfer the dough to a 9-by-13-by-2-inch (23-by-33-by-5-cm) baking dish and press evenly into the bottom and ½ inch (12 mm) up the sides.

3. Bake until lightly browned, 20–25 minutes. Transfer to a wire rack and let cool for 10 minutes.

4. In a large bowl, whisk together the eggs, granulated sugar, lime juice, vanilla, lime zest, and the remaining ¼ cup (1¼ oz/40 g) flour. Pour over the warm baked crust.

5. Return to the oven and bake until the center is set and no longer sticky, 22–24 minutes. The filling will be slightly soft when touched, similar to a custard or pie filling. Transfer to a wire rack and let cool completely. Cover and refrigerate for at least 6 hours or as long as overnight.

6. Just before serving, cut into bars and dust the top with confectioners' sugar. Store any leftovers in the refrigerator, dusting with additional confectioners' sugar before serving.

MAKES 36 BAR COOKIES

NUTRITIONAL ANALYSIS PER COOKIE
Calories 133 (Kilojoules 559); Protein 2 g; Carbohydrates 23 g; Total Fat 4 g; Saturated Fat 2 g; Cholesterol 33 mg; Sodium 15 mg; Dietary Fiber 0 g

Classic Pecan Tart

PASTRY DOUGH

1¼ cups (5 oz/155 g) soft winter-wheat flour, such as White Lily brand, or cake (soft-wheat) flour

½ teaspoon salt

¼ cup (2 oz/60 g) solid vegetable shortening, chilled

¼ cup (2 oz/60 g) chilled unsalted butter, cut into small cubes

3–6 tablespoons (1½–3 fl oz/45–90 ml) ice water

¾ cup (6 oz/185 g) sugar

¾ cup (7½ oz/235 g) light corn syrup

⅓ cup (3 oz/90 g) unsalted butter, melted

3 eggs, lightly beaten

2 tablespoons bourbon (optional)

1 tablespoon grated orange zest

1 teaspoon vanilla extract (essence)

¼ teaspoon salt

1 cup (4 oz/125 g) pecan halves, plus ⅓ cup (1½ oz/45 g) coarsely chopped

The pecan tree grows wild in many areas of the temperate South. On chilly autumn mornings you'll find kids and grown-ups alike scurrying in their yards, bucket in hand, trying to beat the squirrels to this prized nut. Bourbon and orange zest add subtle flavor to this cherished Southern dessert.

1. To make the pastry, in a bowl, stir together the flour and salt. Add the shortening and cut in with a pastry blender, 2 knives, or your fingers until the mixture resembles cornmeal. Add the butter and cut in until it forms tiny balls about the size of peas. Add the ice water, a little at a time, stirring and tossing with the pastry blender or a fork until the mixture holds together. Gather the dough into a ball and flatten into a disk. Wrap in plastic wrap and refrigerate for 30–60 minutes.

2. On a lightly floured work surface, roll out the dough into a round about 11 inches (28 cm) in diameter and ⅛ inch (3 mm) thick. Fold the round into quarters and place in a 10-inch (25-cm) tart pan with a removable bottom. Unfold, then press gently into the bottom and sides of the pan. Trim the overhang even with the pan rim. Refrigerate until ready to fill.

3. Position a rack in the lower third of the oven and preheat to 325°F (165°C).

4. In a bowl, stir together the sugar, corn syrup, melted butter, eggs, bourbon (if using), orange zest, vanilla, salt, pecan halves, and chopped pecans. Pour into the chilled pastry and place on a baking sheet.

5. Bake until the center is slightly soft to the touch, the edges are set, and the crust is golden brown, 45–55 minutes. Transfer to a wire rack to cool for 30 minutes, then remove the pan sides and slide the tart off the pan bottom onto a serving plate. Serve warm or at room temperature.

SERVES 8

NUTRITIONAL ANALYSIS PER SERVING
Calories 543 (Kilojoules 2,281); Protein 5 g; Carbohydrates 60 g; Total Fat 33 g; Saturated Fat 12 g; Cholesterol 118 mg; Sodium 275 mg; Dietary Fiber 1 g

Coconut Layer Cake with Raspberry Filling

½ cup (4 oz/125 g) unsalted butter, at room temperature

1¼ cups (10 oz/310 g) sugar

3 eggs, separated

3 cups (12 oz/375 g) soft winter-wheat flour, such as White Lily brand, or cake (soft-wheat) flour

1 tablespoon baking powder

½ teaspoon salt

1⅓ cups (11 fl oz/340 ml) milk

2 teaspoons vanilla extract (essence)

½ teaspoon coconut extract (essence), optional

¾ cup (7½ oz/235 g) seedless raspberry preserves

4 cups (1 lb/500 g) sweetened shredded coconut

ICING

1⅓ cups (11 oz/345 g) sugar

⅛ teaspoon salt

⅔ cup (5 fl oz/160 ml) water

4 egg whites

1 teaspoon vanilla extract (essence)

¼ teaspoon coconut extract (essence), optional

1. Preheat the oven to 350°F (180°C). Butter two 9-inch (23-cm) round cake pans. Line the bottoms with waxed paper, then butter and flour the waxed paper, tapping out the excess flour.

2. In a bowl, using an electric mixer set on medium-high speed, beat together the butter and 1 cup (8 oz/250 g) of the sugar until light and fluffy. Add the egg yolks, one at a time, beating well after each addition. On a sheet of waxed paper, sift together the flour, baking powder, and salt. Add the flour mixture to the butter mixture in three batches alternately with the milk. Beat in the vanilla and the coconut extracts. In another bowl, beat the egg whites until they form soft peaks. Gradually add the remaining ¼ cup (2 oz/60 g) sugar and beat until the whites are glossy and hold their shape. Stir one-third of the egg whites into the batter. Then fold the batter into the remaining egg whites. Divide between the pans.

3. Bake until a toothpick inserted into the center of a cake comes out clean, about 30 minutes. Let cool in the pans on racks for 5 minutes, then invert onto the racks and let cool completely.

4. To make the icing, in a heavy saucepan over low heat, combine the sugar, salt, and water and stir until the sugar dissolves. Raise the heat to medium-high and bring to a rolling boil. Cook the syrup until it registers 240°F (115°C) on a candy thermometer. Remove from the heat. At this point, in a bowl, begin beating the egg whites on medium-high speed until soft peaks form. Pour the syrup into the egg whites in a thin stream while beating on high speed. Beat until the icing is cooled, thick, and glossy, about 7 minutes. Beat in the vanilla and the coconut extracts.

5. Place 1 cake layer on a serving plate, spread with the raspberry preserves, and top with the second layer. Cover the top and sides of the cake with the icing, and then cover the icing with the coconut. Cover and refrigerate until ready to serve. Refrigerate any leftovers.

SERVES 12

NUTRITIONAL ANALYSIS PER SERVING
Calories 635 (Kilojoules 2,667); Protein 7 g; Carbohydrates 103 g; Total Fat 23 g; Saturated Fat 17 g; Cholesterol 79 mg; Sodium 403 mg; Dietary Fiber 3 g

Orange Angel Food Cake with Berry Sauce

1¼ cups (5 oz/155 g) soft winter-wheat flour, such as White Lily brand, or cake (soft-wheat) flour

1¾ cups (14 oz/435 g) sugar

14 large egg whites

1½ teaspoons cream of tartar

¼ teaspoon salt

2 tablespoons fresh orange juice

1 teaspoon vanilla extract (essence)

grated zest of 2 oranges

SAUCE

⅔ cup (5 oz/155 g) sugar

1 tablespoon cornstarch (cornflour)

1 cup (4 oz/125 g) sliced strawberries

½ cup (2 oz/60 g) raspberries

½ cup (2 oz/60 g) blueberries

⅓ cup (3 fl oz/80 ml) water

2 tablespoons Grand Marnier (optional)

In the South, such light, airy cakes made from stiffly beaten egg whites and no yolks are often referred to simply as angel cake. They are a mainstay of church suppers and bake sales.

1. Position a rack in the lower third of the oven and preheat to 375°F (190°C). Sift together the flour and ¾ cup (6 oz/185 g) of the sugar three times onto a piece of waxed paper. Set aside.

2. In a large bowl, using an electric mixer set at medium-high speed, beat together the egg whites, cream of tartar, and salt until soft peaks form when the beaters are lifted. Gradually beat in the remaining 1 cup (8 oz/250 g) sugar, about 1 tablespoon at a time, until very stiff peaks form. Beat in the orange juice, vanilla, and orange zest.

3. Sift about one-fourth of the flour mixture over the beaten whites. Using a rubber spatula, gently fold the flour into the whites. Repeat this process three times to incorporate all of the flour. Ladle the batter into an ungreased 10-inch (25-cm) tube pan. Run a knife gently through the batter to eliminate any air pockets.

4. Bake until lightly browned, about 35 minutes. Remove from the oven, invert the tube of the pan over the neck of a bottle, and let cool completely. (Some tube pans have feet built around the rim, making the bottle unnecessary.) When cool, gently loosen the edges of the cake with a thin-bladed knife or icing spatula and invert onto a serving platter.

5. While the cake is cooling, make the sauce: In a saucepan over medium-high heat, mix together the sugar, cornstarch, berries, and water. Bring to a boil, reduce the heat to low, and cook until the sauce thickens and is glossy, about 5 minutes. Stir in the Grand Marnier, if using. Let cool.

6. To serve, slice the cake and ladle some sauce over each slice.

SERVES 10

NUTRITIONAL ANALYSIS PER SERVING
Calories 302 (Kilojoules 1,268); Protein 6 g; Carbohydrates 70 g; Total Fat 0 g; Saturated Fat 0 g; Cholesterol 0 mg; Sodium 136 mg; Dietary Fiber 1 g

One of the best Southern traditions is the bake sale, an annual event held to raise money for local churches or temples, women's groups, fraternal lodges, or any one of a slew of different student groups, from the marching band to the debate club.

What is a Southern bake sale? Simply put, the participants bake their best-loved cakes, pies, cookies, and muffins and donate them to their favorite organization, which then displays the baked goods, usually on long tables covered with red-and-white gingham-checked cloths. Children delight in seeing all the treats and quickly gather around the table like famished ants at a picnic.

Cakes and pies are proudly displayed on beautiful glass pedestals, on plates lined with paper lace doilies, or in Tupperware cake carriers. Having been to church suppers, funerals, and anniversary and birthday celebrations, the buyers all know who bakes the best cakes or pies. Once the sale begins, these prized sweets are the first ones snatched up, sometimes causing a squabble among neighbors eager to take home a one-of-a-kind dessert.

Southern **Bake Sale**

Folks often buy two cakes, one for eating as soon as they get home and one for wrapping and freezing, to be brought out later for a special occasion.

Prices vary from a quarter for a plain sugar cookie to five bucks for a pie to ten bucks for a three-tiered coconut cake—all bargains, as far as Southerners are concerned.

Oatmeal Cookies

1 cup (8 oz/250 g) unsalted butter,
  at room temperature

1 cup (7 oz/220 g) firmly packed
  light brown sugar

¾ cup (6 oz/185 g) granulated sugar

1 egg

2 teaspoons vanilla extract (essence)

1½ cups (7½ oz/235 g) all-purpose
  (plain) flour

1 teaspoon baking soda (bicarbonate
  of soda)

1 teaspoon ground cinnamon

½ teaspoon ground cloves

¼ teaspoon salt

freshly grated nutmeg to taste

3 cups (3 oz/90 g) quick-cooking
  rolled oats

1 cup (3 oz/90 g) chopped dried
  apples

1 cup (4 oz/125 g) dried cranberries

1 cup (4 oz/125 g) chopped walnuts

ICING (OPTIONAL)

6 oz (185 g) good-quality white
  chocolate, chopped

1 teaspoon solid vegetable shortening

Some of my most pleasant childhood memories are of eating these warm, chewy, fragrant cookies. Feel free to use a substitute for what you don't have on hand such as raisins for the dried cranberries.

1. Preheat the oven to 375°F (190°C). Line 2 baking sheets with parchment (baking) paper.

2. In a large bowl, combine the butter, brown sugar, and granulated sugar. Using an electric mixer set on medium-high speed, beat until light and fluffy, about 3 minutes. Beat in the egg and then the vanilla. On a sheet of waxed paper, sift together the flour, baking soda, cinnamon, cloves, salt, and nutmeg. Add the flour mixture to the butter mixture and stir with a wooden spoon just until blended. Fold in the oats, apples, cranberries, and walnuts. The batter will be very stiff. Scoop up the dough by tablespoonfuls and place on the prepared baking sheets, spacing them about 2 inches (5 cm) apart.

3. Bake in batches, if necessary, until the edges of the cookies are golden, about 14 minutes. Let cool on the baking sheets on a wire rack for 1 minute, then carefully transfer the cookies to the rack and let cool completely.

4. To make the icing (if using), place the white chocolate and shortening in a heavy-duty lock-top plastic bag and seal closed. Place the bag in a large heatproof bowl. Pour barely simmering water over the bag to cover. Let stand until the chocolate begins to melt, about 3 minutes. Using your hands, knead the chocolate in the bag until smooth. Using scissors, snip off a corner to make a small opening. Drizzle the chocolate over the cooled cookies. Let stand until the chocolate hardens.

5. Eat immediately, or store between layers of waxed paper in an airtight container for up to 2 weeks in the refrigerator.

MAKES ABOUT 42 COOKIES

NUTRITIONAL ANALYSIS PER COOKIE
Calories 167 (Kilojoules 701); Protein 2 g; Carbohydrates 22 g; Total Fat 8 g;
Saturated Fat 4 g; Cholesterol 17 mg; Sodium 55 mg; Dietary Fiber 1 g

White Chocolate Banana Pudding

⅔ cup (5 oz/155 g) plus ¼ cup (2 oz/ 60 g) sugar

3 tablespoons cornstarch (cornflour)

4 cups (32 fl oz/1 l) milk

5 eggs, separated

½ cup (4 fl oz/125 ml) sour cream

1 tablespoon vanilla extract (essence)

1 box (7 oz/220 g) thin Swedish gingersnaps

4 or 5 very ripe bananas, peeled and sliced

6 oz (185 g) coarsely chopped good-quality white chocolate

Said to have been one of Elvis's favorites, this recipe is made with staples from the Southern larder: milk, eggs, sugar, and bananas. I have made this down-home dessert even more luscious by adding sour cream and white chocolate.

1. In a saucepan, combine the ⅔ cup (5 oz/155 g) sugar and the cornstarch. Gradually stir in the milk. Place over medium heat and bring to a gentle boil, stirring constantly. Cook for 1 minute and remove from the heat.

2. Gradually whisk about one-fourth of the hot milk mixture into the egg yolks, then stir the egg yolks back into the saucepan. Return to medium heat and cook, stirring constantly, until the mixture is thick and bubbly, about 5 minutes. Remove from the heat and fold in the sour cream and the vanilla. Cover with plastic wrap, pressing it directly onto the surface of the custard, and let cool completely, about 30 minutes.

3. Preheat the oven to 325°F (165°C). Lightly butter a 2-qt (2-l) baking dish. Arrange half of the gingersnaps in the bottom and along the sides of the baking dish. Top with half of the banana slices and half of the white chocolate. Uncover the cooled custard and whisk until smooth. Pour half of the custard over the white chocolate. Repeat the layering with the remaining ingredients.

4. In a bowl, beat the egg whites with an electric mixer set on medium-high speed until soft peaks form. Add the remaining ¼ cup (2 oz/60 g) sugar, 1 tablespoon at a time, and continue beating until stiff peaks form. Spread the egg white mixture evenly over the custard, bringing it to the edges of the dish.

5. Bake until the meringue is a light golden brown, about 12 minutes. Transfer to a wire rack and let cool for about 35 minutes before serving slightly warm. Alternatively, let cool completely, cover loosely with plastic wrap, and refrigerate until well chilled before serving.

SERVES 8

NUTRITIONAL ANALYSIS PER SERVING
Calories 532 (Kilojoules 2,234); Protein 11 g; Carbohydrates 73 g; Total Fat 23 g; Saturated Fat 13 g; Cholesterol 163 mg; Sodium 365 mg; Dietary Fiber 1 g

Upside-Down Persimmon Gingerbread

¾ cup (6 oz/185 g) unsalted butter

1 cup (7 oz/220 g) firmly packed
dark brown sugar

⅔ cup (2½ oz/75 g) chopped pecans

3 Fuyu persimmons, seeded and
thinly sliced

1½ cups (6 oz/185 g) soft winter-
wheat flour, such as White Lily
brand, or cake (soft-wheat) flour

¾ teaspoon baking soda (bicarbonate
of soda)

2 teaspoons ground ginger

1 teaspoon ground cinnamon

¼ teaspoon ground cloves

¼ teaspoon freshly grated nutmeg

¼ teaspoon salt

1 egg, lightly beaten

¼ cup (3 oz/90 g) dark molasses

1 teaspoon vanilla extract (essence)
mixed with ⅓ cup (3 fl oz/80 ml)
boiling water

In the South, persimmons are available mid-October through December, making this spicy gingerbread a welcome winter-time Dixie dessert. Choose the tomato-shaped Fuyu persimmon for this recipe. It should yield to gentle pressure.

1. Preheat the oven to 350°F (180°C). Lightly coat a well-seasoned 10-inch (25-cm) cast-iron frying pan with vegetable oil.

2. In the frying pan over medium heat, melt ¼ cup (2 oz/60 g) of the butter and ½ cup (3½ oz/110 g) of the brown sugar, stirring until the sugar melts. Add the pecans and persimmons, overlapping them in a circular pattern. Reduce the heat to low and cook, without stirring, about 3 minutes to glaze the persimmons. Remove from the heat.

3. On a piece of waxed paper, sift together the flour, baking soda, ginger, cinnamon, cloves, nutmeg, and salt. In a large bowl, using an electric mixer set at medium-high speed, beat together the remaining ½ cup (4 oz/125 g) butter and ½ cup (3½ oz/110 g) brown sugar until light and fluffy, about 1 minute. Add the egg and molasses and continue to beat until well blended, about 1 minute longer. Gently fold the flour mixture into the butter-sugar mixture in three batches, alternating with the vanilla mixture and beginning and ending with the flour. Do not overmix. Pour over the pecans and the persimmons in the pan.

4. Bake until the cake springs back to the touch, about 30 minutes. Transfer to a wire rack and let cool for 5 minutes. Then invert a serving plate over the frying pan and, holding them firmly together, invert carefully. Lift off the frying pan. Slice the gingerbread into wedges and serve warm.

SERVES 8

NUTRITIONAL ANALYSIS PER SERVING
Calories 433 (Kilojoules 1,819); Protein 4 g; Carbohydrates 53 g; Total Fat 24 g;
Saturated Fat 11 g; Cholesterol 73 mg; Sodium 216 mg; Dietary Fiber 1 g

Mint Julep

MINT SUGAR SYRUP

10 large fresh mint sprigs,
    plus 4 small sprigs for garnish

1 cup (8 fl oz/250 ml) water

1 cup (8 oz/250 g) sugar

crushed ice

1½ cups (12 fl oz/360 ml) aged
    Kentucky bourbon

Although this is the official drink of the annual Kentucky Derby, it is actually drunk all over the South the year-round. Sip it slowly through a short straw to enjoy the pleasant aroma of the fresh mint, which prepares your palate for the potent potion to come.

1. To make the mint sugar syrup, gently tear or crush the 10 mint sprigs with your fingers and place them in a saucepan. Add the water and sugar and bring to a boil over medium heat, stirring occasionally. Reduce the heat to low and simmer, uncovered, for 5 minutes. Remove from the heat and let cool completely. Strain through a sieve, discarding the mint. You will have 2 cups (16 fl oz/500 ml) syrup. (The syrup can be stored in the refrigerator for up to 1 month.)

2. To make the juleps, pour ¼ cup (2 fl oz/60 ml) of the cooled syrup into each of four 10–fl oz (310-ml) goblets or silver cups. Fill to the top with crushed ice. When frost begins to form on the outside, add 3 fl oz (90 ml) of the bourbon to each serving. With an iced-tea spoon or long-handled bar spoon, stir together the syrup, ice, and bourbon. Garnish each serving with a mint sprig and serve at once.

SERVES 4

Mojito

This south Florida delight is infused with the flavor of mint, lime, sugar, and lots of rum, all shipped from Cuba to Miami and surrounding ports in pre-Castro days.

In each of 4 tall 10–fl oz (310-ml) glasses, mix 2 tablespoons each of the mint sugar syrup and lime juice. Add several ice cubes, 3 tablespoons of the rum, and ½ cup (4 fl oz/125 ml) of the soda to each glass. Stir well, then garnish each serving with a lime slice and a mint sprig. Serve at once.

SERVES 4

½ cup (4 fl oz/125 ml) mint sugar
    syrup (above)

½ cup (4 fl oz/125 ml) fresh lime juice

ice cubes

¾ cup (6 fl oz/180 ml) light rum

2 cups (16 fl oz/500 ml) club soda,
    chilled

4 lime slices

4 fresh mint sprigs

Sweet Iced Tea

7 cups (56 fl oz/1.75 l) water

12 tea bags

⅛ teaspoon baking soda

1 cup (8 fl oz/250 ml) mint sugar syrup *(page 136)*, or to taste, made without the mint sprigs

ice cubes

lemon, lime, or orange wedges or fresh mint sprigs

Lovingly referred to as the "house wine of the South," this tall, cool classic is a staple at nearly every Southern gathering. The pinch of baking soda helps to balance the natural acidity in the tea, resulting in a smoother drink. For mint tea, make the sugar syrup with the mint sprigs.

1. In a saucepan, bring 3½ cups (28 fl oz/875 ml) of the water to a rolling boil. Place the tea bags in a heatproof pitcher. Add the baking soda and pour in the boiling water. Let steep for 10–15 minutes; the timing will depend upon how strong you like your tea.

2. Remove and discard the tea bags. Stir in the remaining 3½ cups (28 fl oz/875 ml) water and sugar syrup to taste. Pour over ice cubes and citrus wedges or mint sprigs in tall glasses and serve at once.

MAKES ABOUT 2 QT (2 L)

Lemonade

Whether lounging lazily on a fishing bank (with no bait on your hook) or resting after a busy day of yard work, nothing refreshes the soul quite like an ice-cold glass of lemonade. Limes can be substituted for the lemons for an even tarter temptation. For pink lemonade, add ⅓ cup (3 fl oz/80 ml) cranberry juice cocktail to the pitcher. Test the mix as you add the sugar syrup, to sweeten to your taste.

In a large pitcher, combine the sugar syrup, lemon juice, water, and lemon slices. Pour over ice cubes in tall glasses. Serve immediately.

MAKES 1½ QT (1.5 L)

1 cup (8 fl oz/250 ml) mint sugar syrup *(page 136)*, or to taste, made without the mint sprigs

¾ cup (6 fl oz/180 ml) fresh lemon juice

4 cups (32 fl oz/1 l) water

1 lemon, sliced

ice cubes

Glossary

Andouille Sausage

The name of this pork sausage is a tip-off both to its origins in France and to its popularity in the Creole and Cajun cooking of Louisiana. Although plump and delectably smoky and spicy, America's version is somewhat less hot than the French original, with the heat counter-balanced by the sweetness of the cane syrup used to baste the sausage during smoking. Andouille commonly is used as a seasoning in hearty dishes like gumbo or jambalaya, although it may also be grilled whole and featured at breakfast, lunch, or dinner.

Apple Cider

Apple orchards have long flourished throughout the South, and freshly pressed sweet and fermented hard ciders have been popular there since colonial days. They are enjoyed as thirst-quenching drinks or as flavoring elements in both savory and sweet recipes.

Bacon Drippings

In many old-fashioned Southern kitchens, a can or crock stands beside or at the back of the stove, ready to receive drip-pings poured off from frying pans in which bacon has been cooked. Rich in sweet-smoky flavor, this fat, also known as bacon grease, is traditionally saved and used to fry eggs, corn pones, catfish, and other favorite dishes.

Bourbon

The form of whiskey known as bourbon is a distinctly Southern product *(page 85)*. Most often drunk neat to savor its smooth, smoky taste, bourbon also features in such traditional Southern cocktails as the Sazerac, a New Orleans favorite; the old-fashioned, invented at Louisville's Pendennis Club; and the mint julep, the traditional thirst quencher at the Kentucky Derby. It also flavors many recipes in the South. Good bourbon is widely available in liquor and food stores. Maker's Mark and Knobb Creek are well regarded among brands.

Buttermilk

Early Irish, Scottish, and English settlers introduced the habit of drinking butter-milk, the tangy, yellow-flecked liquid pro-duced when milk is churned to make butter. Today, a well-chilled glass of but-termilk remains a favorite Southern pick-me-up, especially when paired with corn bread. Its thick consistency and rich taste also make it an excellent ingredient in both savory and sweet recipes, and its acidity frequently gives an extra lift to quick breads and pancake batters. Most buttermilk now sold in food stores is "cultured" by the addition of bacteria that transform the milk into a product resembling the hand-churned version.

Catfish

Distinguished by the long, very sharp whiskerlike feelers that inspire its fanci-ful name, this scale-free fish has long thrived in the rivers, streams, creeks, bayous, ponds, and reservoirs of the South. Despite its ugly appearance, the catfish, sometimes referred to as "cat," has sweet, tender white flesh that is widely savored. In recent decades, con-cerns over polluted waters have given rise to farm-raised catfish, which also lack the lingering hint of muddy flavor that some consumers found unpleasant in their wild cousins.

Chicory

The roasted and ground roots of a bitter, leafy green, chicory is mixed with and used to stretch coffee. Café du Monde, a well-known New Orleans establishment, is famous for its chicory-infused coffee.

Grits

Taking their name from the Middle English *gyrt,* meaning bran, the term *grits* in the South refers specifically to hominy grits, coarsely ground from dried kernels of hulled mature white corn. Grits are available in several forms: stone-ground grits, which take about 40 minutes to cook; regular coarse-grained grits, which take about 20 minutes to cook; quick-cooking grits, which have a finer texture and cook in 3 to 5 minutes; and instant grits, which have been pre-cooked and dried, sacrificing some flavor and texture for the sake of speed. All over the South, grits are served with breakfast eggs and cured meats, as well as a side dish with lunch or dinner.

Hush Puppies

Said to be named for the practice of tossing them to the dogs to keep the critters from howling while dinner was cooking, these crunchy balls of deep-fried corn bread are popularly sold at snack stands throughout the South. To make your own, start with the corn bread recipe on page 92, omitting the oil, sage leaves, butter, and corn. Add 1 small finely chopped onion and decrease the buttermilk to 1¼ cups (10 fl oz/310 ml). Deep-fry in oil or fat heated to 375°F (190°C) until golden brown.

Key Lime

Unlike the familiar, larger, somewhat elongated Persian variety more commonly found in food stores, the Key lime is distinguished by its thin, yellow skin and juicy, aromatic, sweet-sour flesh. Although residents of the Florida Keys claim the Key lime as their own, featuring the juice in the pie of the same name, these distinctive limes are, in fact, similar to the limes grown in Mexico and are increasingly available in food stores.

Chiles

BANANA

Its long, slender form and bright yellow color give this variety its name. Usually mild and sweet, banana peppers are most often used for pickling, although they are also eaten raw in salads.

BIRD'S EYE

Varying from hot to sweet, these peppers resemble cherries, under which name they are often sold.

CHIPOTLE

The fully ripened, smoke-dried form of the jalapeño, this chile adds hot, aromatic flavor to savory dishes. Chipotles are sold packaged loose in cellophane wrappers, canned in vinegar, or canned in a thick vinegar-based sauce and labeled *en adobo.*

DRIED HOT

The term most often applies to a small, slender, dried red chile that resembles the Mexican serrano variety and may be found in cellophane packages labeled *Japones.* Other small, dried hot varieties include the árbol, chiltepin, chilipiquin. and Thai.

FINGER HOT

Also known as the Korean chile, this medium-hot variety is about the size of a finger—3–4 inches (7–10 cm) long and about ¾ inch (2 cm) in diameter. It's the chile of choice for hot-pepper vinegar.

JALAPEÑO

This familiar, fiery chile has thick, juicy flesh and a tapered body up to 3 inches (7.5 cm) long. Most often sold in its immature green form, the jalapeño is increasingly available ripe and red.

MILD GREEN

Most commonly refers to long, green, mildly hot chiles variously known as Anaheim, Arizona, or New Mexico chiles, depending upon where they are grown; or, in Spanish, *chile verde.*

SCOTCH BONNET

A close cousin to the habañero, this highly aromatic variety is thought to be a thousand times more fiery than the jalapeño. It is popular throughout Latin America.

SERRANO

This hot, little, slender chile, native to the mountainous regions of northern Mexico, is widely used in both its immature green and ripened red forms.

Mayonnaise

Although it is most commonly sold in the South today under the English spelling, this rich emulsion of egg yolks and oil is still sometimes referred to as mahonaise in the Deep South, reflecting the region's French roots. This spelling refers to Mahon, on the island of Minorca, where the chef who catered to Marechal de Richelieu reputedly invented mayonnaise in 1756. Throughout the South, mayonnaise is popularly used in salad dressings and sandwich spreads. It is also the basis for tartar sauce and is lent pungency with garlic to make aioli, or "High Holy" mayonnaise. Duke's, a popular Southern brand, is made with egg yolks and has no sugar added.

Mirliton

On the outside, this native fruit resembles a plump, ridged, pale yellow to light green pear. Its hard shell conceals crisp white flesh that cooks to a tender consistency and delicate flavor reminiscent of summer squashes. Also known outside the South by such names as vegetable pear, mango squash, chayote, christophene, and chocho, mirlitons are usually peeled, cut up, and cooked like other squashes; or they are halved like avocados, stuffed, and baked or steamed.

Okra

Native to Africa, okra was brought to the South by slaves. The slender, tapered, gray-green pods grow up to 9 inches (23 cm) long, but they are best eaten small, young, and tender. They have crisp exterior flesh, slightly gummy interiors, and an earthy, slightly acidic flavor. Okra is outstanding when pickled or deep-fried, and it also adds body to such stews as the burgoo of Kentucky and Louisiana's gumbos, which take their name from the original African word for okra, *ngombo* or *kingombo*. Although fresh okra is at its peak in summer, the vegetable also freezes well and can be found in the frozen-foods section of most markets.

Oysters

Cool waters along the South's Atlantic and Gulf shores have long harbored many fine varieties of oyster. Some of the most popular varieties include the Chincoteagues found off Delaware, Maryland, and Virginia; Florida's coon oysters, so called because they're favorites of raccoons living in the mangrove swamps where they grow; those harvested on the Gulf of Mexico in Florida's Apalachicola Bay; the Bon Secour oysters of Mobile, Alabama; and the large, plump oysters harvested in Lake Ponchartrain, near New Orleans. That city, in particular, is famous for its appreciation of oysters, whether eaten raw from the shells, or fried and stuffed into French loaves to make po' boys, once considered a poor man's feast.

Peaches

Although Georgia is known as the "peach state," South Carolina leads the South in peach production. Peaches, *Prunus persica,* are believed to be native to China, coming to North America via Persia and Europe.

Pecans

The seeds of a hickory tree native to Mississippi and Alabama, pecans were long ago enjoyed by the region's Chickasaw, Choctaw, and Natchez tribes. In fact, in some parts of the South, they were known as Natchez nuts, as well as by such variations on their common spelling as peccans and pecawns. Harvested in the fall, the sweet, crunchy nutmeats, which resemble elongated walnuts, store well in their shells for up to nine months in the freezer or up to two months at cool room temperature. Although sometimes ground to use as a thickener for stews, most often they are showcased in candies and desserts, from pralines and brittles to pecan pies.

Pepper Jelly

Perhaps borrowing from the British tradition of making savory-sweet mint jelly to serve with roast lamb, Southerners have long enjoyed jams made from hot chiles combined with vinegar, sugar, and pectin, along with a dash of red or green food coloring to give the clear jelly a pepperlike hue. Whether homemade or bought in well-stocked food stores, the sweet, tart, spicy preserves are traditionally eaten as an hors d'oeuvre or snack atop cream cheese smeared on a cracker. Pepper jelly also makes a wonderful glaze or condiment for country ham.

Pones

The term most commonly describes corn bread batter that has been shaped into small, oval mounds and then fried on a griddle or baked. The word derives from the Indian *appone,* which refers to corn kernels that have been hulled to make hominy.

Pot Likker

Pot likker is served ladled over the greens or corn bread or enjoyed on its own as a soup. So revered is pot likker that notorious Louisiana governor Huey Long referred to it as "the noblest dish the mind of man has yet conceived."

Sorghum Syrup

Also called sorghum molasses, sorghum syrup is akin to cane syrup, produced and used in similar ways. Sorghum is a cereal grass, its stalks holding the sweet juice from which the syrup is made. It's used in baking and as a sweet condiment on the Southern table.

Sweet Potato

Southerners favor the deep orange–fleshed variety of this tuber over its pale-fleshed cousin more common in the North. Both types fall under the botanical classification *Ipomoea batatas,* a relative of the morning glory. Despite the fact that Southerners refer to their sweet potatoes as "yams," these sweet potatoes are unrelated to the much larger and blander true yams of the Caribbean. Whatever they call them, Southerners prepare sweet potatoes in many ways, including simply roasted in the ashes of the hearth, then slit opened and enriched with butter; mashed, like regular potatoes; or sweetened and spiced as a filling for sweet potato pie.

Tomatoes, Green

A traditional country specialty, unripe green tomatoes have a firm texture and sharp, acidic taste that makes them ideal candidates for turning into pickles or relishes, or for slicing and coating with seasoned flour and cornmeal, then frying in bacon drippings as a side dish for breakfast, lunch, or dinner.

Vinegars

Sharp tasting and fragrant, vinegars are integral components of the Southern pantry. They are used in pickling and salad dressings, as well as to add a distinctive edge of flavor to savory and, sometimes, sweet recipes. Cider vinegar is often enjoyed for the sweet hint of apple flavor it conveys. Sliced or chopped hot chiles are steeped in relatively bland white vinegar to make pepper vinegar, a popular ingredient and condiment.

Seasonings

CAYENNE PEPPER

A source of heat in many regional dishes, including Creole and Cajun favorites, this fine brownish red powder is ground from the dried small, hot red chile of the same name.

CRAWFISH AND CRAB BOIL

This traditional commercial blend of seasonings is added to a pot of boiling water in which crustaceans are about to be cooked, seasoning them as they simmer. The mixture usually includes bay leaf, dried chile, and clove, among other seasonings.

CREOLE

Term applied to a New Orleans–style blend of seasonings that, depending upon the brand, might typically include such ingredients as paprika, cayenne pepper, allspice, cumin, black pepper, lemon zest, and thyme.

FILÉ POWDER

Made from the bark of the sassafras tree, filé powder is a thickening agent and is most commonly used to thicken gumbo. It can also be sprinkled, sparingly, on a dish to lend a very particular earthy flavor.

JAMAICAN JERK

Lively commercial or homemade blend of Caribbean-inspired sweet hot seasonings that commonly combine such ingredients as allspice, sugar, chile, garlic, ginger, clove, bay leaf, black pepper, lime juice, and even a splash of rum.

LEMON BALM

Also known by such other names as balm mint and melissa, this gentle herb has a distinctive lemon scent and is most often used in omelets, salads, soups, game dishes, and punches.

MINT

This refreshing herb grows wild in the South and was long favored as a seasoning by the Choctaw tribe. In today's South, it probably reaches its apotheosis crushed in the refreshing iced bourbon drink known as the mint julep.

SESAME SEED

This tiny, ivory-colored, teardrop-shaped seed is still often referred to in the South as benne, the name it was called by the slaves who first brought it here from Africa in the 16th century. Sesame seeds are particularly popular in coastal South Carolina and Georgia, where they were first planted, and lend rich, nutty flavor to dishes ranging from stews and breads to cakes, cookies, and candies.

Index

Acknowledgments

Ray Overton wishes to thank his grandmother, Louise Harris, for introducing him to the ways of the Southern kitchen; Nathalie Dupree for teaching and training him along the way; Virginia Willis for her dear friendship; and Val Cipollone for the hand-holding that made this book a reality.

Leigh Beisch wishes to thank The New Lab and Pro Camera, San Francisco, CA, and FUJI Film for their generous support of this project.

Weldon Owen wishes to thank the following people and associations for their generous assistance and support
in producing this book: Desne Border, Ken DellaPenta, Christine DePedro, Dana Goldberg, Wendely Harvey, Niki Krause,
Annette Sandoval, Big 6 Farm, Bland Farms, Hill Nutrition Associates, Past Present, and Smithfield Packing.

Photo Credits

Weldon Owen wishes to thank the following photographers and organizations for permission to reproduce their copyrighted photographs:
Pages 14–15 (Clockwise from top left) : Russell Kaye; Melanie Acevedo; Dana Gallagher; Mark Sherman/Aristock; Simon Watson; Jeff Greenberg/Index Stock
Page 16: Ron Mellott/Index Stock; Richard Bowditch; Gordon Kilgore/Aristock
Page 36: Russell Kaye; Simon Watson; Madeline Polss; Laurie Smith
Page 74: Sonja Lashua/Transparencies; Jeff Greenberg/Index Stock; Madeline Polss; Laurie Smith
Page 108: Robb Helfrick/Aristock; Ben Asen/Envision; Kelly Culpepper

Time-Life Books is a division of Time Life Inc.

Time-Life is a trademark of Time Warner Inc.,
and affiliated companies.

TIME LIFE INC.

President and CEO: **Jim Nelson**

TIME-LIFE TRADE PUBLISHING

Vice President and Publisher: **Neil Levin**

Senior Director of Acquisitions
and Editorial Resources: **Jennifer L. Pearce**

WILLIAMS-SONOMA

Founder and Vice-Chairman: **Chuck Williams**

Associate Book Buyer: **Cecilia Michaelis**

WELDON OWEN INC.

Chief Executive Officer: **John Owen**

President: **Terry Newell**

Chief Operating Officer: **Larry Partington**

Vice President International Sales: **Stuart Laurence**

Managing Editor: **Val Cipollone**

Copy Editor: **Sharon Silva**

Consulting Editor: **Norman Kolpas**

Design: **Jane Palecek**

Production Director: **Stephanie Sherman**

Production Editor: **Sarah Lemas**

Food Stylist: **George Dolese**

Prop Stylist: **Sara Slavin**

Studio Assistant: **Sheri Giblin**

Food Styling Assistant: **Leslie Busch**

Scenic Photo Research: **Caren Alpert**

The Williams-Sonoma New American Cooking Series
conceived and produced by Weldon Owen Inc.
814 Montgomery Street, San Francisco, CA 94133

In collaboration with Williams-Sonoma
3250 Van Ness Avenue, San Francisco, CA 94109

Separations by Bright Arts Graphics (S) Pte. Ltd.
Printed in Singapore by Tien Wah Press (Pte.) Ltd.

A WELDON OWEN PRODUCTION
Copyright © 2000 Weldon Owen Inc. and
Williams-Sonoma Inc.
All rights reserved, including the right of
reproduction in whole or in part in any form.

Map copyright © Ann Field

First printed in 2000
10 9 8 7 6 5 4 3 2 1

Library of Congress
Cataloging-in-Publication Data

Overton, Ray L.
The South / general editor, Chuck Williams; recipes and
text by Ray Overton; photography by Leigh Beisch.
p. cm. — (Williams-Sonoma New American Cooking)
ISBN 0-7370-2040-7
1. Cookery, American--Southern style. I. Williams,
Chuck. II. Title. III. Series.
TX715.2,S65094 2000
641.5975— dc21   99-43383
CIP

A NOTE ON NUTRITIONAL ANALYSIS
Each recipe is analyzed for significant nutrients per
serving. Not included in the analysis are ingredients
that are optional or added to taste, or are suggested
as an alternative or substitution either in the recipe
or in the recipe introduction. In recipes that yield
a range of servings, the analysis is for the middle
of that range.

A NOTE ON WEIGHTS AND MEASURES
All recipes include customary U.S. and metric
measurements. Metric conversions are based on
a standard developed for these books and have
been rounded off. Actual weights may vary.